PASS THE NEW YORK NOTARY PUBLIC EXAM 2010 EDITION

Angelo Tropea

ISBN 1449581560

Published by Angelo Tropea, P.O. Box 26271, Brooklyn, NY 11202-6271

Please note that the unofficial sections of statutes (New York State Law) and accompanying "highlights" are edited and are presented solely for the purpose of quick study aids and not as legal reference. The primary sources of legal reference are the laws themselves which are available in many places, including online at:

http://public.leginfo.state.ny.us/menuf.cgi

Notaries Public...hold an office which can trace its origins back to ancient Rome when they were called *scribae, tabellius* or *notarius*. They are easily the oldest continuing branch of the legal profession worldwide.

Wikipedia.org

For information on acquiring the

Pass the New York Notary Public Exam

Computer Program

visit www.NotaryProgram.com

Additional information about this interactive computer software
which includes the sections of law specified for the notary public
exam may be found on page 256 of this book.

CONTENTS

THE AIM OF THIS BOOK

The NYS Department of State, Division of Licensing Services, has published an excellent booklet, "Notary Public License Law." It contains all the sections of law you need to pass the Notary Public Exam and to be a well informed and professional notary public. The aim of this book is to complement the official publication by highlighting the more important sections of law and offering study tools to help you better prepare for the exam and become a more knowledgeable and professional practicing notary public.

THIS BOOK PROVIDES:

1. Edited sections of NYS law on the scope of the NYS Notary Public Exam as announced by the Department of State.

2. Law highlights to stress and clarify legal facts and areas that are most relevant to notary public candidates.

3. True/False, fill-in and other "Quick Questions" to help you remember facts and definitions.

4. Multiple choice questions to help you practice for the notary public exam.

5. Practice exams to help you to further solidify your knowledge of the laws relevant to notaries.

We believe that the combination of the above will provide the tools and the required practice to help you achieve your goal of passing the notary public exam and also increase your understanding and appreciation of laws important to notaries public.

For detailed information on how to apply for the NYS Notary Public Exam, please visit:

http://www.dos.state.ny.us/lcns/listoflncs.htm

HOW TO USE THIS BOOK

There are probably as many ways to study successfully as there are people. However, in the more than twenty-five years preparing study materials and conducting classes for civil service exams, I have found that certain methods seem to work better than others with the great majority of students. The following are time tested suggestions that you might want to consider as you incorporate this book in the study plan that is best for you.

SUGGESTIONS:

1. First read the law highlights. They are generally in simpler English than the edited statutes.

2. After reading the highlights, read the edited statutes for a deeper understanding. (The statutes are unofficial and edited in places.)

3. Try the "Quick Questions" (4 on a page). Do not go on to the multiple choice questions until you have mastered these questions. Read the comments after each answer to reinforce important facts.

4. Now tackle the multiple choice questions (2 on page). On the actual test you will have around 40 multiple choice questions.

5. When you think you are ready, take Practice Exam 1, then Practice Exam 2.

Whenever you answer a question incorrectly, review that section of law. Also, make sure you are confident with all the legal terms. They will form the basis of your understanding of the law. Study every day. Take this book with you – and make it your friend.

The actual NYS statutes are available in many places, including online at:

http://public.leginfo.state.ny.us/menuf.cgi

NOTARY PUBLIC LAWS

EXECUTIVE LAW

ELECTION LAW

PUBLIC OFFICERS LAW

REAL PROPERTY LAW

Section	Description and Page Number
290	Definitions and effect of article/38
298	Acknowledgments and proofs within the state/38
302	Acknowledgments and proofs by married women/40
303	Requisites of acknowledgments/40
304	Proof by subscribing witness/40
306	Certificate of acknowledgment of proof/40
309-a	Uniform forms of certificates of acknowledgment of proof within the state/42
309-b	Uniform forms of certificates of acknowledgment or proof without the state/44
330	Officers guilty of malfeasance liable for damages/48
333	Recording of conveyances of real property/48

JUDICIARY LAW

484	None but attorneys to practice in the state/50
485	Violation of certain preceding sections a misdemeanor/52
750	Power of courts to punish for criminal contempts/52

PENAL LAW

70.00	Sentence of imprisonment for felony/54
70.15	Sentences of imprisonment for misdemeanors and violations/54
170.10	Forgery in the second degree/54
175.40	Issuing a false certificate/54
195.00	Official misconduct/56

COUNTY LAW

534	County Clerk; appointments of notaries public/56

BANKING LAW

335	(Safe deposit boxes)/58

CIVIL PRACTICE LAW AND RULES

3113	(Persons before whom depositions may be taken/60

DOMESTIC RELATIONS LAW

11	(Marriages)/60

LEGAL TERMS

	("Acknowledgment" to "Will")/62

<u>REMINDER</u>

1. First read the law highlights. They are generally in simpler English than the edited statutes.

2. After reading the highlights, read the edited statutes for a deeper understanding.

(The statutes are unofficial and edited in places.)

After a review of the law, you will be ready to use the study cards (flash cards) to help you reinforce your understanding and memory of the law.

Study deep…

It will not only help you
pass the exam, but it will also help you
become a more knowledgeable,
respected and professional notary public!

LAW

Executive Law 130: Appointment of notaries public

The Secretary of State may appoint and commission as many notaries public for the State of New York as in his or her judgment may be deemed best, whose jurisdiction shall be co-extensive with the boundaries of the state.

The appointment of a notary public shall be for a term of 4 years.

An application for an appointment as notary public shall be in form and set forth such matters as Secretary of State shall prescribe.

Every person appointed as notary public must, at the time of his or her appointment, be a citizen of the United States and either a resident of the State of New York or have an office or place of business in New York State.

A notary public who is a resident of the State and who moves out of the state but still maintains a place of business or an office in New York State does not vacate his or her office as a notary public. A notary public who is a nonresident and who ceases to have an office or place of business in NYS, vacates his or her office as a notary public. A notary public who is a resident of New York State and moves out of the state and who does not retain an office or place of business in this State shall vacate his or her office as a notary public.

A non-resident who accepts the office of notary public in this State thereby appoints the Secretary of State as the person upon whom process can be served on his or her behalf.

Before issuing to any applicant a commission as notary public, unless he or she be an attorney and counselor at law duly admitted to practice in this state or a court clerk of the Unified Court System who has been appointed to such position after taking a Civil Service promotional examination in the court clerk series of titles, the Secretary of State shall satisfy himself or herself that the applicant is of good moral character, has the equivalent of a common school education and is familiar with the duties and responsibilities of a notary public;

<u>HIGHLIGHTS</u>

Executive Law 130: Appointment of notaries public

Notaries public are appointed by the Secretary of State (NYS).

Notaries have statewide jurisdiction (authority).

The term of a notary is 4 years.

The Secretary of State determines the notary public application.

To be eligible for appointment, a notary must be a citizen of the United States, AND be a NYS resident (OR have a place of business in NYS).

Notary (NYS resident) may move outside NYS state and still be a notary IF he maintains a place of business or office in NYS.

A NYS resident who moves out of NYS and non-resident who does NOT maintain an office or place of business in NYS vacates his office as a notary.

A non-resident notary appoints the (NYS) Secretary of State as the designated person to whom process can be served.

The Secretary of State must be satisfied that the notary applicant is:

1. of good moral character AND

2. has the equivalent of a common school educations AND

3. is familiar with duties and responsibilities of a notary.

    (This does NOT apply to attorneys and certain Court Clerks).

LAW

provided, however, that where a notary public applies, before the expiration of his or her term, for reappointment with the county clerk or where a person whose term as notary public shall have expired applies within 6 months thereafter for reappointment as a notary public with the county clerk, such qualifying requirements may be waived by the Secretary of State,

and further, where an application for reappointment is filed with the county clerk after expiration of the aforementioned renewal period by a person who failed or was unable to re-apply by reason of his or her induction or enlistment in the armed forces of the United States, such qualifying requirements may also be waived by the Secretary of State, provided such application for reappointment is made within a period of 1 year after the military discharge of the applicant under conditions other than dishonorable.

In any case, the appointment or reappointment of any applicant is in the discretion of the Secretary of State.

The Secretary of State may suspend or remove from office, for misconduct, any notary public appointed by him or her

but no such removal shall be made unless the person who is sought to be removed shall have been served with a copy of the charges against him or her and have an opportunity of being heard.

No person shall be appointed as a notary public under this article who has been convicted, in NYS or any other state or territory, of a felony or any of the following offenses, to wit:

(a) illegally using, carrying or possessing a pistol or other dangerous weapon;

(b) making or possessing burglar's instruments;

(c) buying or receiving or criminally possessing stolen property;

(d) unlawful entry of a building;

(e) aiding escape from prison;

(f) unlawfully possessing or distributing habit forming narcotic drugs;

HIGHLIGHTS

Does not apply to a person applying for reappointment:

1. during his term as notary, or

2. within 6 months of expiration of term as notary.

Also, the Secretary of State may waive such requirements in any case.

The Secretary of State may waive such requirements for a person not able to apply for reappointment because of his service in the U.S. armed forces, provided that his discharge is not dishonorable and applies within 1 year of his discharge.

The appointment or reappointment of any applicant is in the discretion of the Secretary of State.

The Secretary of State may suspend or remove from office, for misconduct, any notary public.

However, must first give the person a copy of the charges and an opportunity to be heard.

A person convicted of a felony or any of the following charges CANNOT be appointed a notary.

(a) illegally using, carrying or possessing a pistol or dangerous weapon;

(b) making or possessing burglar's instruments;

(c) buying or receiving or criminally possessing stolen property;

(d) unlawful entry of a building;

(e) aiding escape from prison;

(f) unlawfully possessing or distributing habit forming narcotic drugs;

LAW

(g) violating 270, 270-a, 270-b, 270-c, 271, 275, 276, 550, 551, 551-a and subdivisions 6, 8, 10 or 11 of 722 of the former Penal Law as in force and effect immediately prior to September 1, 1967, or violating 165.25, 165.30, subdivision 1 of 240.30, subdivision 3 of 240.35 of the Penal Law, or violating 478, 479, 480, 481, 484, 489 and 491 of the Judiciary Law; or

(h) vagrancy or prostitution, and who has not subsequent to such conviction received an executive pardon therefore or a certificate of good conduct from the parole board to remove disability under this section because of such conviction.

A person regularly admitted to practice as an attorney and counselor in the courts of record of this state, whose office for the practice of law is within the State, may be appointed a notary public and retain his office as such notary public although he resides in or removes to an adjoining state.

For the purpose of this and the following sections of this article such person shall be deemed a resident of county where he maintains such office.

Study hint:

Try reading the "highlights" first before you read the edited law. The "highlights" will give you a quick "bird's eye view" of the legal area before you immerse yourself in legal terminology.

<u>HIGHLIGHTS</u>

(g) violating sections of the old penal law, or current penal law, or specified sections of the Judiciary Law.

(h) vagrancy or prostitution (unless received an executive pardon or a certificate of good conduct from the parole board).

An attorney admitted to practice in NYS may be appointed a notary (and if he moves outside NYS may still remain a notary if he retains an office in NYS).

The above attorney is considered a resident of the county where he has an office.

Remember:

The "highlights" are not intended to interpret or provide a comprehensive distillation of the law. They are meant to point out areas that will aid your understanding and retention of important facts.

LAW

Executive Law 131: Procedure of appointment; fees and commissions

1. Applicants for a notary public commission shall submit to Secretary of State with their application the oath of office, duly executed before any person authorized to administer an oath, together with their signature.

2. Upon being satisfied of the competency and good character of applicants for appointment as notaries public, the Secretary of State shall issue a commission to such persons; and the official signature of the applicants and the oath of office filed with such applications shall take effect.

3. The Secretary of State shall receive a non-refundable application fee of $60 from applicants for appointment, which fee shall be submitted together with the application. No further fee shall be paid for the issuance of the commission.

4. A notary public identification card indicating the appointee's name, address, county and commission term shall be transmitted to the appointee.

5. The commission, duly dated, and a certified copy or the original of the oath of office and the official signature, and $20 apportioned from the application fee shall be transmitted by the Secretary of State to the county clerk in which the appointee resides by the 10th day of the following month.

6. The county clerk shall make a proper index of commissions and official signatures transmitted to that office by the Secretary of State pursuant to the provisions of this section.

7. Applicants for reappointment of a notary public commission shall submit to county clerk with their application the oath of office, duly executed before any person authorized to administer an oath, together with their signature.

8. Upon being satisfied of the completeness of the application for reappointment, the county clerk shall issue a commission to such persons; and the official signature of the applicants and the oath of office filed with such applications shall take effect.

HIGHLIGHTS

Executive Law 131: Procedure of appointment; fees and commissions

1. A notary public applicant must submit to the Secretary of State:

    a. notary public application

    b. oath of office (duly executed, with signature)

2. The Secretary of State, if satisfied as to competency and good moral character of the applicant, shall issue a commission to the applicant.

3. The application fee for notary public is $60.

4. The notary I.D. card given to the applicant shall indicate the name, address, county and commission term.

5. By the 10th day of the following month, the Secretary of State shall transmit to the county clerk: 1) the commission, 2) certified copy of original oath of office with signature, 3) $20 from the $60 fee paid by the applicant.

6. The county clerk must maintain an index of commissions.

7. Applicants for reappointment must submit to the county clerk 1) application, 2) oath of office (duly executed, with signature)

8. The county clerk, if satisfied as to completeness of the **application for reappointment**, shall issue a commission to the applicant.

LAW

9. The county clerk shall receive a non-refundable application fee of $60 from each applicant for reappointment, which fee shall be submitted together with the application.

No further fee shall be paid for the issuance of the commission.

10. The commission, duly dated, and a certified or original copy of the application, and $40 apportioned from the application fee plus interest as may be required by statute shall be transmitted by the county clerk to the Secretary of State by the 10th day of the following month.

11. The Secretary of State shall make a proper record of commissions transmitted to that office by the county clerk pursuant to the provisions of this section.

12. Except for changes made in an application for reappointment, Secretary of State shall receive a non-refundable fee of $10 for changing the name or address of a notary public.

13. The Secretary of State may issue a duplicate identification card to a notary public for one lost, destroyed or damaged upon application therefore on a form prescribed by the Secretary of State and upon payment of a non-refundable fee of $10.

Each such duplicate identification card shall have the word "duplicate" stamped across the face thereof, and shall bear the same number as the one it replaces.

Executive Law 132: Certificates of official character of notaries public

The secretary of state or county clerk of the county in which the commission of a notary public is filed may certify to the official character of such notary public and any notary public may file his autograph signature and a certificate of official character in the office of any county clerk of any county in the state and in any register's office in any county having a register and thereafter such county clerk may certify as to the official character of such notary public. The secretary of state shall collect for each certificate of official character issued by him the sum of ten dollars. The county clerk and register of any county with whom a certificate of official

HIGHLIGHTS

9. The application fee for reappointment is $60 and is given to the county clerk.

10. By the 10th day of the following month, the county clerk shall transmit to the Secretary of State: 1) the commission, 2) certified copy of original of the application, 3) $40 from the $60 fee paid by the applicant (and interest, if applicable).

11. The Secretary of State shall keep a record of commissions it receives from the county clerk.

12. The Secretary of State fee for changing the name or address of a notary public is $10 (except where the change is made in the application for reappointment).

13. The fee for a duplicate notary identification card (replacement for one lost, destroyed or damaged) is $10.

A duplicate notary I.D. card must have the word "duplicate" stamped on its face and must have the same number as the card it replaces.

Executive Law 132: Certificates of official character of notaries public

Certificate of official character of a notary public may be issued by:

1. Secretary of State

2. county clerk

Certificate certifies as to the official character of a notary public.

County clerk **filing fee** for a certificate of official character is $10.

The fee for the **issuance by the county clerk** of a certificate of official character with seal attached is $5.

LAW

character has been filed shall collect for filing the same the sum of ten dollars. For each certificate of official character issued, with seal attached, by any county clerk, the sum of five dollars shall be collected by him.

Executive Law 133: Certification of notarial signatures

The county clerk of a county in whose office any notary public has qualified or has filed his autograph signature and a certificate of his official character, shall, when so requested and upon payment of a fee of $3 affix to any certificate of proof or acknowledgment or oath signed by such notary anywhere in the state of New York, a certificate under his hand and seal, stating that a commission or a certificate of his official character with his autograph signature has been filed in his office, and that he was at time of taking such proof or acknowledgment or oath duly authorized to take the same; that he is well acquainted with the handwriting of such notary public or has compared the signature on the certificate of proof or acknowledgment or oath with the autograph signature deposited in his office by such notary public and believes that the signature is genuine.

An instrument with such certificate of authentication of county clerk affixed thereto shall be entitled to be read in evidence or to be recorded in any of the counties of this state in respect to which a certificate of a county clerk may be necessary for either purpose.

Executive Law 134: Signature and seal of county clerk

The signature and seal of a county clerk, upon a certificate of official character of a notary public or the signature of a county clerk upon a certificate of authentication of the signature and acts of a notary public or commissioner of deeds, may be a facsimile, printed, stamped, photographed or engraved thereon.

HIGHLIGHTS

Executive Law 133: Certification of notarial signatures

A county clerk may affix a certificate of official character to any certificate or proof or acknowledgment or oath signed by a notary. The fee for the certification of the notarial signature is $3.

An instrument with such a certificate may be read in evidence or recorded in NYS where a certificate of a county clerk may be necessary for either purpose.

Executive Law 134: Signature and seal of county clerk

The signature and seal of a county clerk on the certificate of official character or certificate of authentication of the signature of a notary public may be: facsimile, printed, stamped, photographed or engraved.

LAW

Executive Law 135: Powers and duties, in general, of notaries public who are attorneys at law

Every notary public duly qualified is hereby authorized and empowered within and throughout NYS to administer oaths and affirmations, to take affidavits and depositions, to receive and certify acknowledgments or proof of deeds, mortgages and powers of attorney and other instruments in writing; to demand acceptance or payment of foreign and inland bills of exchange, promissory notes and obligations in writing, and to protest the same for non-acceptance or non-payment, as the case may require, and, for use in another jurisdiction, to exercise such other powers and duties as by the laws of nations and according to commercial usage, or by the laws of any other government or country may be exercised and performed by notaries public, provided that when exercising such powers he shall set forth the name of such other jurisdiction.

A notary public who is an attorney at law regularly admitted to practice in NYS may, in his discretion, administer an oath or affirmation to or take the affidavit or acknowledgment of his client in respect of any matter, claim, action or proceeding.

For any misconduct by a notary public in the performance of any of his powers such notary public shall be liable to the parties injured for all damages sustained by them.

A notary public shall not, directly or indirectly, demand or receive for the protest for the non-payment of any note, or for the non-acceptance or non-payment of any bill of exchange, check or draft and giving the requisite notices and certificates of such protest, including his notarial seal, if affixed thereto, any greater fee or reward than seventy-five cents for such protest, and ten cents for each notice, not exceeding five, on any bill or note.

Every notary public having a seal shall, except as otherwise provided, and when requested, affix his seal to such protest free of expense.

HIGHLIGHTS

Executive Law 135: Powers and duties, in general, of notaries public who are attorneys at law

Notaries have the power in NYS to:

1. administer oaths and affirmations

2. take affidavits and depositions

3. receive and certify acknowledgments or proofs of deeds, mortgages, and powers of attorney and other written instruments

4. demand acceptance or payment of foreign and inland bills of exchange, promissory notes and written obligations

5. protest the items in #4 above for non-acceptance or non payment for use in another jurisdiction

6. exercise powers as may be exercised by notaries public in other jurisdictions.

An attorney who is a notary public may administer an oath or affirmation or take an affidavit or acknowledgment of his client.

A notary public is liable to an injured party for damages sustained by them as a result of his misconduct.

Fee for protest of note, commercial paper, etc. / $.75

Fee for each additional Notice of Protest (limit 5) / $.10

LAW

Executive Law 135-a: Notary public or commissioner of deeds; acting without appointment; fraud in office

1. Any person who holds himself out to the public as being entitled to act as a notary public or commissioner of deeds, or who assumes, uses or advertises the title of notary public or commissioner of deeds, or equivalent terms in any language, in such a manner as to convey the impression that he is a notary public or commissioner of deeds without having first been appointed as notary public or commissioner of deeds, or

2. A notary public or commissioner of deeds, who in the exercise of the powers, or in the performance of duties of such office shall practice any fraud or deceit, the punishment for which is not otherwise provided for by this act, shall be guilty of a misdemeanor.

Executive Law 136: Notarial fees

A notary public shall be entitled to the following fees:

1. For administering an oath or affirmation, and certifying the same when required, except where another fee is specifically prescribed by statute, two dollars.

2. For taking and certifying the acknowledgment or proof of execution of a written instrument, by one person, two dollars, and by each additional person, two dollars, for swearing each witness thereto, two dollars.

Executive Law 137: Statement as to authority of notaries public

In exercising his powers pursuant to this article, a notary public, in addition to the venue of his act and his signature, shall print, typewrite, or stamp beneath his signature in black ink, his name, the words "Notary Public State of New York, " the name of the county in which he originally qualified, and the date upon which his

HIGHLIGHTS

Executive Law 135-a: Notary public or commissioner of deeds; acting without appointment; fraud in office

A person who acts as a notary or commissioner of deeds without first being appointed is guilty of a misdemeanor.

A notary or commissioner of deeds who commits fraud or deceit as a notary or commissioner of deeds is guilty of a misdemeanor.

Executive Law 136: Notarial fees

Notarial fees:

Oath or affirmation / $2

Acknowledgment (each person) / $2

Proof of execution (each person) / $2

Swearing witness / $2

Executive Law 137: Statement as to authority of notaries public

When a notary exercises his powers, he must:

Write the venue and sign the form, and in addition must print, typewrite or stamp in black ink the following beneath his signature:

1. his name

LAW

commission expires and, in addition, wherever required, a notary public shall also include the name of any county in which his certificate of official character is filed, using the words "Certificate filed .... County. " A notary public who is duly licensed as an attorney and counselor at law in this state may in his discretion, substitute the words "Attorney and Counselor at Law" for the words "Notary Public. " A notary public who has qualified or who has filed a certificate of official character in the office of the clerk in a county or counties within the city of New York must also affix to each instrument his official number or numbers in black ink, as given to him by the clerk or clerks of such county or counties at the time such notary qualified in such county or counties and, if the instrument is to be recorded in an office of the register of the city of New York in any county within such city and the notary has been given a number or numbers by such register or his predecessors in any county or counties, when his autographed signature and certificate are filed in such office or offices pursuant to this chapter, he shall also affix such number or numbers. No official act of such notary public shall be held invalid on account of the failure to comply with these provisions. If any notary public shall willfully fail to comply with any of provisions of this section, he shall be subject to disciplinary action by the secretary of state. In all the courts within this state the certificate of a notary public, over his signature, shall be received as presumptive evidence of the facts contained in such certificate; provided, that any person interested as a party to a suit may contradict, by other evidence, the certificate of a notary public.

Executive Law 138: Powers of notaries public or other officers who are stockholders, directors, officers or employees of a corporation

A notary public, justice of the supreme court, a judge, clerk, deputy clerk, or special deputy clerk of a court, an official examiner of title, or mayor or recorder of a city, a justice of the peace, surrogate, special surrogate, special county judge, or commissioner of deeds,

HIGHLIGHTS

2. the words "Notary Public State of New York"

3. the name of the county in which he originally qualified

4. the date upon which his commission expires

5. in addition, wherever required, must include the name of any county in which his certificate of official character is filed, using the words "Certificate filed .... County."

6. If the notary is also an attorney, he may substitute the words "Attorney and Counselor at Law" for the words "Notary Public."

7. If the notary qualified in New York City or filed a certificate of official character in the City of New York, he shall also affix to each instrument his official number(s) in black ink.

An official act of such notary public shall not be held invalid on account of the failure to comply with these provisions.

If any notary willfully fails to comply with any provisions of this section, he shall be subject to disciplinary action by the secretary of state.

In all NYS courts the certificate of a notary public, over his signature, shall be received as evidence of the facts contained in such certificate; provided, that any person interested as a party to a suit may contradict, by other evidence, the certificate of a notary public.

Executive Law 138: Powers of notaries public or other officers who are stockholders, directors, officers or employees of a corporation

A notary or commissioner of deeds who is a stockholder, director, officer or employee of a corporation may take the acknowledgment or proof or administer an oath to any party to a written instrument executed to or by such corporation, or may protest for non-

LAW

who is a stockholder, director, officer or employee of a corporation may take the acknowledgment or proof of any party to a written instrument executed to or by such corporation, or administer an oath to any other stockholder, director, officer, employee or agent of such corporation, and such notary public may protest for non-acceptance or non-payment, bills of exchange, drafts, checks, notes and other negotiable instruments owned or held for collection by such corporation; but none of the officers above named shall take the acknowledgment or proof of a written instrument by or to a corporation of which he is a stockholder, director, officer or employee, if such officer taking such acknowledgment or proof be a party executing such instrument, either individually or as representative of such corporation, nor shall a notary public protest any negotiable instruments owned or held for collection by such corporation, if such notary public be individually a party to such instrument, or have a financial interest in the subject of same. All such acknowledgments or proofs of deeds, mortgages or other written instruments, relating to real property heretofore taken before any of the officers aforesaid are confirmed. This act shall not affect any action or legal proceeding now pending.

Executive Law 140:

14. No person who has been removed from office as a commissioner of deeds for the city of New York, as hereinbefore provided, shall thereafter be eligible again to be appointed as such commissioner nor, shall he be eligible thereafter to appointment to office of notary public.

15. Any person who has been removed from office as aforesaid, who shall, after knowledge of such removal, sign or execute any instrument as a commissioner of deeds or notary public shall be deemed guilty of a misdemeanor.

HIGHLIGHTS

payment bills of exchange, drafts, checks, notes and other negotiable instruments owned or held by such corporation.

However, cannot do so if the notary or commissioner of deeds is a party or has a beneficial interest in the subject.

Executive Law 140:

14. A person removed from the office of commissioner of deeds (NYC) is not eligible for appointment as commissioner of deeds or as a notary public.

15. A person so removed who executes or signs any instrument as a notary or commissioner of deeds is guilty of a misdemeanor.

LAW

Executive Law 142-a: Validity of acts of notaries public and commissioners of deeds notwithstanding certain defects

1. Except as provided in subdivision three of this section, official certificates and other acts heretofore or hereafter made or performed of notaries public and commissioners of deeds heretofore or hereafter and prior to the time of their acts appointed or commissioned as such shall not be deemed invalid, impaired or in any manner defective, so far as they may be affected, impaired or questioned because of defects described in subdivision 2.

2. This section shall apply to the following defects:

(a) ineligibility of the notary public or commissioner of deeds to be appointed or commissioned as such;

(b) misnomer or misspelling of name or other error made in his appointment or commission;

(c) omission of the notary public or commissioner of deeds to take or file his official oath or otherwise qualify;

(d) expiration of his term, commission or appointment;

(e) vacating of his office by change of his residence, by acceptance of another public office, or by other action on his part;

(f) the fact that the action was taken outside the jurisdiction where the notary public or commissioner of deeds was authorized to act.

3. No person shall be entitled to assert the effect of this section to overcome a defect described in subdivision two if he knew of the defect or if the defect was apparent on the face of the certificate of the notary public or commissioner of deeds; provided however, that this subdivision shall not apply after the expiration of six months from the date of the act of the notary public or commissioner of deeds.

4. After the expiration of six months from the date of the official certificate or other act of the commissioner of deeds, subdivision one of this section shall be applicable to a defect consisting in omission of the certificate of a commissioner of deeds to state the date on which and the place in which an act was done, or consisting of an error in such statement.

HIGHLIGHTS

Executive Law 142-a: Validity of acts of notaries public and commissioners of deeds notwithstanding certain defects

1. Generally, a notary public act shall NOT be deemed invalid, impaired or defective due to...

2. ...the following defects:

(a) ineligibility of notary or commissioner of deeds to be appointed or commissioned;

(b) misnomer or misspelling of name or other error in appointment or commission;

(c) omission of the notary public or commissioner of deeds to take or file his official oath or otherwise qualify;

(d) expiration of his term, commission or appointment;

(e) vacating of his office because of change of his residence, acceptance of another public office, or other reason;

(f) the fact that the action was taken outside the jurisdiction of the notary public or commissioner of deeds.

3. Generally, above cannot be asserted if the defect was apparent or person knew of the defect (shall not apply after the expiration of 6 months from act of notary or commissioner of deeds).

4. After 6 months of act, sub 1 shall be applicable to defect in omission of the certificate of a commissioner of deeds to state date and place in which act was done, or an error in such statement.

LAW

5. This section does not relieve any notary public or commissioner of deeds from criminal liability imposed by reason of his act, or enlarge the actual authority of any such officer, nor limit any other statute or rule of law by reason of which the act of a notary public or commissioner of deeds, or the record thereof, is valid or is deemed valid in any case.

Election Law 3-200:

3-200: 4. No person shall be appointed as election commissioner or continue to hold office who is not a registered voter in the county and not an enrolled member of party recommending his appointment, or who holds any other public office, except that of commissioner of deeds, notary public, village officer, city or town justice, member of a community board within the city of New York or trustee or officer of a school district outside of a city.

Public Officers Law 3:

No person shall be capable of holding a civil office… who shall have been or shall be convicted of a violation of the selective draft act of the United States, enacted May eighteenth, nineteen hundred seventeen, or the acts amendatory or supplemental thereto, or of the federal selective training and service act of nineteen hundred forty or the acts amendatory thereof or supplemental thereto.

Public Officers Law 10: Official oaths

An oath of office may be administered by a judge of the court of appeals, the attorney general, or by any officer authorized to take, within the state, the acknowledgment of the execution of a deed of real property, or by an officer in whose office the oath is required to be filed.

<u>HIGHLIGHTS</u>

5. This section does not relieve any notary or commissioner of deeds from criminal liability.

Election Law 3-200:

Both a commissioner of elections and an inspector of elections are eligible to be notaries public.

Public Officers Law 3:

A person convicted of a violation of any of the following is not eligible to be a notary public:

1. selective draft act of U.S. (1917)

2. acts amending this draft act

3. selective training and service act (1940)

Public Officers Law 10: Official oaths

A notary public may administer an oath of office.

LAW

Public Officers Law 67: Fees of public officers

1. Each public officer upon whom a duty is expressly imposed by law, must execute same without fee or reward, except where a fee or other compensation therefore is expressly allowed by law.

2. An officer or other person, to whom a fee or other compensation is allowed by law, for any service, shall not charge or receive a greater fee or reward, for that service, than is so allowed.

3. An officer, or other person, shall not demand or receive any fee or compensation, allowed to him by law for any service, unless the service was actually rendered by him; except that an officer may demand in advance his fee, where he is, by law, expressly directed or permitted to require payment thereof, before rendering the service.

4…An officer or other person, who violates either of the provisions contained in this section, is liable, in addition to the punishment prescribed by law for the criminal offense, to an action in behalf of the person aggrieved, in which the plaintiff is entitled to treble damages.

Public Officers Law 69: Fee for administering certain official oaths prohibited

An officer is not entitled to a fee, for administering the oath of office to a member of the legislature, to any military officer, to an inspector of election, clerk of the poll, or to any other public officer or public employee.

<u>HIGHLIGHTS</u>

Public Officers Law 67: Fees of public officers

1. A public officer can collect a fee only if provided by law.

2. Can only collect specified fee (not greater amount).

3. Can only demand or receive a fee for services rendered or as specified by law.

4. Violation of above subjects violator to punishment prescribed by law, removal, and treble (triple) damages.

Public Officers Law 69: Fee for administering certain official oaths prohibited

An officer is not entitled to a fee for administering an oath to:

1. a member of the legislature

2. a military officer

3. an inspector of election

4. a clerk of the poll

5. any officer or public employee

LAW

Real Property Law 290: Definitions and effect of article

3. The term "conveyance" includes every written instrument, by which any estate or interest in real property is created, transferred, mortgaged or assigned, or by which title to any real property may be affected, including an instrument in execution of a power, although the power be one of revocation only, and an instrument postponing or subordinating a mortgage lien; except a will, a lease for a term not exceeding three years, an executory contract for the sale or purchase of lands, and an instrument containing a power to convey real property as the agent or attorney for the owner of such property.

Real Property Law 298: Acknowledgments and proofs within the state

The acknowledgment or proof, within this state, of a conveyance of real property situate in this state may be made:

1. At any place within the state, before (a) a justice of the supreme court; (b) an official examiner of title; (c) an official referee; or (d) a notary public.

2. Within the district wherein such officer is authorized to perform official duties, before (a) a judge or clerk of any court of record; (b) a commissioner of deeds outside of the city of New York, or a commissioner of deeds of the city of New York within the five counties comprising the city of New York; (c) the mayor or recorder of a city; d) a surrogate, special surrogate, or special county judge; or (e) the county clerk or other recording officer of a county.

3. Before a justice of the peace, town councilman, village police justice or a judge of any court of inferior local jurisdiction, anywhere within county containing the town, village or city in which he is authorized to perform official duties.

HIGHLIGHTS

Real Property Law 290: Definitions and effect of article

1. The term **"conveyance"** includes a written instrument, by which any estate or interest in real property is created, transferred, mortgaged or assigned, or by which the title to any real property may be affected, including an instrument in execution of a power, and an instrument postponing or subordinating a mortgage lien.

2. It does **not** include a will, a lease for a term not exceeding 3 years, an executory contract for the sale or purchase of lands, and an instrument containing a power to convey real property as the agent or attorney for the owner of such property.

Real Property Law 298: Acknowledgments and proofs within the state

The acknowledgment or proof, within NYS, of a conveyance of real property situate in NYS may be made:

1. **AT ANY PLACE IN NYS**, before

(a) a justice of the supreme court;

(b) an official examiner of title;

(c) an official referee; or (d) a notary public.

2. **WITHIN THE DISTRICT wherein such officer is authorized to perform official duties**, before

(a) a judge or clerk of any court of record;

(b) a commissioner of deeds outside of the city of NY, or a commissioner of deeds of the city of NY within the 5 counties of the city of NY;

(c) the mayor or recorder of a city;

d) a surrogate, special surrogate, or special county judge; or

(e) the county clerk or other recording officer of a county.

3. **WITHIN THE COUNTY containing the town, village or city in which he is authorized to perform official duties** before a justice of the peace, town councilman, village police justice or a judge of any court of inferior local jurisdiction.

LAW

Real Property Law 302: Acknowledgments and proofs by married women

Acknowledgment or proof of a conveyance of real property, within the state, or of any other written instrument, may be made by a married woman the same as if unmarried.

Real Property Law 303: Requisites of acknowledgments

An acknowledgment must not be taken by any officer unless he knows or has satisfactory evidence, that the person making it is the person described in and who executed such instrument.

Real Property Law 304: Proof by subscribing witness

When execution of a conveyance is proved by a subscribing witness, such witness must state his own place of residence, and if his place of residence is in a city, the street and street number, if any thereof, and that he knew the person described in and who executed the conveyance. The proof must not be taken unless the officer is personally acquainted with such witness, or has satisfactory evidence that he is the same person, who was a subscribing witness to the conveyance.

Real Property Law 306: Certificate of acknowledgment of proof

A person taking the acknowledgement or proof of a conveyance must indorse thereupon or attach thereto, a certificate, signed by himself, stating all the matters required to be done, known, or proved on the taking of such acknowledgement or proof; together with the name and substance of the testimony of each witness examined before him, and if a subscribing witness, his place of residence.

HIGHLIGHTS

Real Property Law 302: Acknowledgments and proofs by married women

A married or unmarried woman may make an acknowledgment or proof of a conveyance of real property in NYS.

Real Property Law 303: Requisites of acknowledgments

An officer who takes an acknowledgment must have satisfactory evidence that the person making it is the person described in and who executed the instrument.

Real Property Law 304: Proof by subscribing witness

A subscribing witness must:

1. state his place of residence (street and street number, if in a city)

2. state he knew the person described therein and who executed the conveyance.

The officer must be:

1. acquainted with the witness, or

2. have satisfactory evidence that the witness is same person who is the subscribing witness to the conveyance.

Real Property Law 306: Certificate of acknowledgment of proof

Certificate of acknowledgement or proof must be attached to the conveyance and must have endorsed on it the signature of the person taking the acknowledgment along with the name and substance of the testimony of each witness examined by him, and if a subscribing witness, his place of residence.

LAW

Real Property Law 309-a: Uniform forms of certificates of acknowledgment or proof within this state

1. The certificate of an acknowledgment, within this state, of a conveyance or other instrument in respect to real property situate in this state, by a person, must conform substantially with the following form, the blanks being properly filled:

State of New York)

)ss.:

County of …..........)

On the .... day of .... in the year ..... before me, the undersigned, personally appeared ...., personally known to me or proved to me on the basis of satisfactory evidence to be the individual(s) whose name(s) is (are) subscribed to the within instrument and acknowledged to me that he/she/they executed the same in his/her/their capacity(ies), and that by his/her/their signature(s) on the instrument, the individual(s), or the person upon behalf of which the individual(s) acted, executed the instrument.

(Signature and office of individual taking acknowledgement.)

2. The certificate for a proof of execution by a subscribing witness, within this state, of a conveyance or other instrument made by any person in respect to real property situate in this state, must conform substantially with the following form, the blanks being properly filled:

State of New York)

)ss.:

County of ....)

On the .... day of ...... in the year .... before me, the undersigned, personally appeared ......, the subscribing witness to the foregoing instrument, with whom I am personally acquainted, who, being by me duly sworn, did depose and say that he/she/they reside(s) in ......(if the place of residence is in a city, include the street and street number, if any, thereof); that he/she/they know(s)..........to be the individual described in and who executed the foregoing instrument;

HIGHLIGHTS

Real Property Law 309-a: Uniform forms of certificates of acknowledgment or proof within this state

1. Instruments relating to real property situated in NYS must conform to the following (with blanks filled out):

State of New York)

)ss.:

County of ....)

On the .... day of .... in the year ..... before me, the undersigned, personally appeared ...., personally known to me or proved to me on the basis of satisfactory evidence to be the individual(s) whose name(s) is (are) subscribed to the within instrument and acknowledged to me that he/she/they executed the same in his/her/their capacity(ies), and that by his/her/their signature(s) on the instrument, the individual(s), or the person upon behalf of which the individual(s) acted, executed the instrument.

(Signature and office of individual taking acknowledgement.)

2. The certificate for a proof of execution by a subscribing witness, in NYS of an instrument relating to real property in NYS, must conform to the following (with blanks filled out).

State of New York)

)ss.:

County of ....)

On the .... day of ...... in the year .... before me, the undersigned, personally appeared ......, the subscribing witness to the foregoing instrument, with whom I am personally acquainted, who, being by me duly sworn, did depose and say that he/she/they reside(s) in ......(if the place of residence is in a city, include the street and street number, if any, thereof); that he/she/they know(s)..........to be the individual described in and who executed the foregoing instrument;

LAW

that said subscribing witness was present and saw said ....execute the same; and that said witness at the same time subscribed his/her/their name(s) as a witness thereto.

(Signature and office of individual taking proof.)

3. A certificate of an acknowledgement or proof taken under section three hundred of this article shall include the additional information required by that section.

4. For the purposes of this section, the term "person" means any corporation, joint stock company, estate, general partnership (including any registered limited liability partnership or foreign limited liability partnership), limited liability company (including a professional service limited liability company), foreign limited liability company (including a foreign professional service limited liability company), joint venture, limited partnership, natural person, attorney in fact, real estate investment trust, business trust or other trust, custodian, nominee or any other individual or entity in its own or any representative capacity.

Real Property Law 309-b. Uniform forms of certificates of acknowledgement or proof without this state.

1. The certificate of an acknowledgement, without this state, of a conveyance or other instrument with respect to real property situate in this state, by a person, may conform substantially with the following form, the blanks being properly filled:

State, District of Columbia,   )

Territory, Possession, or   )ss.:

Foreign Country   ):

On the _____ day of _____ in the year _____ before me, the undersigned, personally appeared _____, personally known to me or proved to me on the basis of satisfactory evidence to be the individual(s) whose name(s) is (are) subscribed to the within instrument and acknowledged to me that he/she/they executed the same in his/her/their capacity(ies), and that by his/her/their signature(s) on the instrument, the

HIGHLIGHTS

that said subscribing witness was present and saw said ....execute the same; and that said witness at the same time subscribed his/her/their name(s) as a witness thereto.

(Signature and office of individual taking proof.)

3. A certificate of an acknowledgement or proof taken under section three hundred of this article shall include the additional information required by that section.

4. For the purposes of this section, the term "person" means any corporation, joint stock company, estate, general partnership (including any registered limited liability partnership or foreign limited liability partnership), limited liability company (including a professional service limited liability company), foreign limited liability company (including a foreign professional service limited liability company), joint venture, limited partnership, natural person, attorney in fact, real estate investment trust, business trust or other trust, custodian, nominee or any other individual or entity in its own or any representative capacity.

Real Property Law 309-b. Uniform forms of certificates of acknowledgement or proof without this state.

1. The certificate of an acknowledgement, without this state, of a conveyance or other instrument with respect to real property situate in this state, by a person, may conform substantially with the following form, the blanks being properly filled:

State, District of Columbia,   )

Territory, Possession, or   )ss.:

Foreign Country   ):

On the _____ day of _____ in the year _____ before me, the undersigned, personally appeared _____, personally known to me or proved to me on the basis of satisfactory evidence to be the individual(s) whose name(s) is (are) subscribed to the within instrument and acknowledged to me that he/she/they executed the same in his/her/their capacity(ies), and that by his/her/their signature(s) on the instrument, the

LAW

individual(s), or the person upon behalf of which the individual(s) acted, executed the instrument.

(Signature and office of individual taking acknowledgement.)

2. The certificate for a proof of execution by a subscribing witness, without this state, of a conveyance or other instrument made by any person in respect to real property situate in this state, may conform substantially with the following form, the blanks being properly filled:

State, District of Columbia,)

Territory, Possession, or)ss.:

Foreign Country):

On the _____ day of _____ in the year _____ before me, the undersigned, personally appeared _____, the subscribing witness to the foregoing instrument, with whom I am personally acquainted, who, being by me duly sworn, did depose and say that he/she resides in _____ (if the place of residence is in a city, include the street and street number, if any, thereof); that he/she knows _____ to be the individual described in and who executed the foregoing instrument; that said subscribing witness was present and saw said _____ execute the same; and that said witness at the same time subscribed his/her name as a witness thereto.

(Signature and office of individual taking proof.)

3. No provision of this section shall be construed to:

(a) modify the choice of laws afforded by sections two hundred ninety-nine-a and three hundred one-a of this article pursuant to which an acknowledgement or proof may be taken;

(b) modify any requirement of section three hundred seven of this article;

(c) modify any requirement for a seal imposed by subdivision one of section three hundred eight of this article;

HIGHLIGHTS

individual(s), or the person upon behalf of which the individual(s) acted, executed the instrument.

(Signature and office of individual taking acknowledgement.)

2. The certificate for a proof of execution by a subscribing witness, without this state, of a conveyance or other instrument made by any person in respect to real property situate in this state, may conform substantially with the following form, the blanks being properly filled:

State, District of Columbia,)

Territory, Possession, or   )ss.:

Foreign Country   ):

On the _____ day of _____ in the year _____ before me, the undersigned, personally appeared _____, the subscribing witness to the foregoing instrument, with whom I am personally acquainted, who, being by me duly sworn, did depose and say that he/she resides in _____ (if the place of residence is in a city, include the street and street number, if any, thereof); that he/she knows _____ to be the individual described in and who executed the foregoing instrument; that said subscribing witness was present and saw said _____ execute the same; and that said witness at the same time subscribed his/her name as a witness thereto.

(Signature and office of individual taking proof.)

3. No provision of this section shall be construed to:

(a) modify the choice of laws afforded by sections two hundred ninety-nine-a and three hundred one-a of this article pursuant to which an acknowledgement or proof may be taken;

(b) modify any requirement of section three hundred seven of this article;

(c) modify any requirement for a seal imposed by subdivision one of section three hundred eight of this article;

LAW

4. A certificate of an acknowledgement or proof taken under section three hundred of this article shall include the additional information required by that section.

5. For the purposes of this section, the term "person" means a person as defined in subdivision four of section three hundred nine-a of this article.

6. The inclusion within the body (other than the jurat) of a certificate of acknowledgment or proof made under this section of the city or other political subdivision and the state or country or other place the acknowledgment was taken shall be deemed a non-substantial variance from the form of a certificate authorized by this section.

Real Property Law 330: Officers guilty of malfeasance liable for damages

An officer authorized to take the acknowledgment or proof of a conveyance or other instrument, or to certify such proof or acknowledgment, or to record the same, who is guilty of malfeasance or fraudulent practice in execution of any duty prescribed by law in relation thereto, is liable in damages to the person injured.

Real Property Law 333: Recording of conveyances of real property

2. A recording officer shall not record or accept for record any conveyance of real property, unless said conveyance in its entirety and the certificate of acknowledgment or proof and the authentication thereof, other than proper names therein which may be in another language provided they are written in English letters or characters, shall be in the English language, or unless such conveyance, certificate of acknowledgment or proof, and the authentication thereof be accompanied by and have attached thereto a translation in the English language duly executed and acknowledged by the person or persons making such conveyance and proved and authenticated, if need be, in the manner required of conveyances for recording in this state, or, unless such conveyance,

LAW

4. A certificate of an acknowledgement or proof taken under section 300 of this article shall include the additional information required by that section.

5. For the purposes of this section, the term "person" means a person as defined in subdivision 4 of section 309-a of this article.

6. The inclusion within the body (other than the jurat) of a certificate of acknowledgment or proof made under this section of the city or other political subdivision and the state or country or other place the acknowledgment was taken shall be deemed a non-substantial variance from the form of a certificate authorized by this section.

Real Property Law 330: Officers guilty of malfeasance liable for damages

An officer (notary public) who is guilty of malfeasance or fraudulent practice is liable in damages to the person injured.

Real Property Law 333: Recording of conveyances of real property

2. A recording officer shall not record or accept for record any conveyance of real property, unless the conveyance and the certificate of acknowledgment or proof and the authentication (except for proper names which may be in another language provided they are written in English letters or characters) shall be in English, or unless such conveyance, certificate of acknowledgment or proof, and the authentication be accompanied by and have attached thereto a translation in English duly executed and acknowledged by the person or persons making such conveyance and proved and authenticated, if need be, in the manner required of conveyances for recording in NYS, or, unless such conveyance,

LAW

certificate of acknowledgment or proof, and the authentication thereof be accompanied by and have attached thereto a translation in the English language made by a person duly designated for such purpose by the county judge of the county where it is desired to record such conveyance or a justice of the supreme court and be duly signed, acknowledged and certified under oath or upon affirmation by such person before such judge, to be a true and accurate translation and contain a certification of the designation of such person by such judge.

Judiciary Law 484: None but attorneys to practice in the state

No natural person shall ask or receive, directly or indirectly, compensation for appearing for a person other than himself as attorney in any court or before any magistrate, or for preparing deeds, mortgages, assignments, discharges, leases or any other instruments affecting real estate, wills, codicils, or any other instrument affecting the disposition of property after death, or decedents' estates, or pleadings of any kind in any action brought before any court of record in this state, or make it a business to practice for another as an attorney in any court or before any magistrate unless he has been regularly admitted to practice, as an attorney or counselor, in the courts of record in the state; but nothing in this section shall apply (1) to officers of societies for the prevention of cruelty to animals, duly appointed, when exercising the special powers conferred upon such corporations under section fourteen hundred three of the not-for-profit corporation law; or (2) to law students who have completed at least two semesters of law school or persons who have graduated from law school, who have taken the examination for admittance to practice law in the courts of record in the state immediately available after graduation from law school, or the examination immediately available after being notified by the board of law examiners that they failed to pass said exam, and who have not been notified by the board of law examiners that they have failed to pass two such examinations, acting under the supervision of a legal aid organization, when such students and persons are acting under a program approved by the appellate division of the supreme court of the department in which

HIGHLIGHTS

certificate of acknowledgment or proof, and the authentication thereof be accompanied by and have attached thereto a translation in the English language made by a person duly designated for such purpose by the county judge of the county where it is desired to record such conveyance or a justice of the supreme court and be duly signed, acknowledged and certified under oath or upon affirmation by such person before such judge, to be a true and accurate translation and contain a certification of the designation of such person by such judge.

Judiciary Law 484: None but attorneys to practice in the state

A notary public cannot act as a lawyer.

This section does not apply to:

1. officers of societies for the prevention of cruelty (Section 1403 of the Not-for-Profit Corporation Law).

2. certain law students

3. certain law school graduates.

LAW

the principal office of such organization is located and specifying the extent to which such students and persons may engage in activities prohibited by this statute; or (3) to persons who have graduated from a law school approved pursuant to the rules of the court of appeals for the admission of attorneys and counselors-at-law and who have taken the examination for admission to practice as an attorney and counselor-at-law immediately available after graduation from law school or the examination immediately available after being notified by the board of law examiners that they failed to pass said exam, and who have not been notified by the board of law examiners that they have failed to pass two such examinations, when such persons are acting under the supervision of the state or a subdivision thereof or of any officer or agency of the state or a subdivision thereof, pursuant to a program approved by the appellate division of the supreme court of the department within which such activities are taking place and specifying the extent to which they may engage in activities otherwise prohibited by this statute and those powers of the supervising governmental entity or officer in connection with which they may engage in such activities.

Judiciary Law 485: Violation of certain preceding sections a misdemeanor

Any person violating provisions of sections four hundred seventy-eight, four hundred seventy-nine, four hundred eighty, four hundred eighty-one, four hundred eighty-two, four hundred eighty-three or four hundred eighty-four, shall be guilty of a misdemeanor.

Judiciary Law 750: Power of courts to punish for criminal contempts

B. .... the supreme court has power under this section to punish for a criminal contempt any person who unlawfully practices or assumes to practice law; and a proceeding under this subdivision may be instituted on the court's own motion or on the motion of any officer charged with the duty of investigating or prosecuting unlawful practice of law, or by any bar association incorporated under the laws of this state.

<u>HIGHLIGHTS</u>

To repeat:

A notary public cannot act as a lawyer.

This section does not apply to:

1. officers of societies for the prevention of cruelty (Section 1403 of the Not-for-Profit Corporation Law).

2. certain law students

3. certain law school graduates.

Judiciary Law 485: Violation of certain preceding sections a misdemeanor

Violation of section 484 is a misdemeanor.

Judiciary Law 750: Power of courts to punish for criminal contempts

B. …. the supreme court has power to punish for a criminal contempt any person who unlawfully practices or assumes to practice law.

A proceeding under may be instituted on the court's own motion or on the motion of any officer charged with the duty of investigating or prosecuting unlawful practice of law, or by any bar association incorporated under the laws of this state.

LAW

Penal Law 70.00: Sentence of imprisonment for a felony

Maximum term of indeterminate sentence is at least 3 years.

D felony not to exceed 7 years, E felony not to exceed 4 years

Penal Law 70.15: Sentences of imprisonment for misdemeanors and violation

1. Class A misdemeanor

A sentence of imprisonment for a class A misdemeanor shall be a definite sentence. When such a sentence is imposed the term shall be fixed by the court, and shall not exceed one year....

Penal Law 170.10: Forgery in the second degree

A person is guilty of forgery in the second degree when, with intent to defraud, deceive or injure another, he falsely makes, completes or alters a written instrument which is or purports to be, or which is calculated to become or to represent if completed:

1. A deed, will, codicil, contract, assignment, commercial instrument, credit card, as that term is defined in subdivision seven of section 155.00, or other instrument which does or may evidence, create, transfer, terminate or otherwise affect a legal right, interest, obligation or status; or

2. A public record, or an instrument filed or required or authorized by law to be filed in or with a public office or public servant; or

3. A written instrument officially issued or created by a public office, public servant or governmental instrumentality; or (4) and (5).

Forgery in the second degree is a class D felony.

Penal Law 175.40: Issuing a false certificate

A person is guilty of issuing a false certificate when, being a public servant authorized by law to make or issue official certificates or other official written instruments, and with intent to defraud, deceive or injure another person, he issues such an instrument, or makes the same with intent that it be issued, knowing that it contains a false statement or false information.

Issuing a false certificate is a class E felony.

HIGHLIGHTS

Penal Law 70.00: Sentence of imprisonment for a felony

Maximum term of indeterminate sentence is at least 3 years.

D felony not to exceed 7 years, E felony not to exceed 4 years

Penal Law 70.15: Sentences of imprisonment for misdemeanors and violation

1. Class A misdemeanor

Imprisonment for an A misdemeanor shall be a definite sentence. It shall be fixed by the court, and shall not exceed 1 year....

Penal Law 170.10: Forgery in the second degree

A person is commits forgery in second degree when he falsely makes, completes or alters a written instrument which is or purports to be, or which is calculated to become or to represent if completed:

1. A deed, will, codicil, contract, assignment, commercial instrument, credit card, as defined in subdivision 7 of section 155.00, or other instrument which does or may evidence, create, transfer, terminate or otherwise affect a legal right, interest, obligation or status; or

2. A public record, or an instrument filed or required or authorized by law to be filed in or with a public office or public servant; or

3. A written instrument officially issued or created by a public office, public servant or governmental instrumentality; or (4) and (5).

Forgery in the second degree is a class D felony.

Penal Law 175.40: Issuing a false certificate

A person is guilty of issuing a false certificate when, being a public servant authorized by law to make or issue official certificates or other official written instruments, he issues such an instrument, or makes the same with intent that it be issued, knowing that it contains a false statement or false information.

Issuing a false certificate is a class E felony.

LAW

Penal Law 195.00: Official misconduct

A public servant is guilty of official misconduct when, with intent to obtain a benefit or deprive another person of a benefit:

1. He commits an act relating to his office but constituting an unauthorized exercise of his official functions, knowing that such act is unauthorized; or

2. He knowingly refrains from performing a duty which is imposed upon him by law or is clearly inherent in the nature of his office.

Official misconduct is a class A misdemeanor.

OTHER MISCELLANEOUS LAWS

County Law 534: County Clerk; appointments of notaries public

Each county clerk shall designate from among the members of his or her staff at least one notary public to be available to notarize documents for the public in each county clerk's office during normal business hours free of charge. Each individual appointed by the county clerk to be a notary public pursuant to this section shall be exempt from the examination fee and application fee required by section one hundred thirty-one of the executive law.

HIGHLIGHTS

Penal Law 195.00: Official misconduct

A public servant (notary public) is guilty of official misconduct when, with intent to obtain a benefit or deprive another person of a benefit:

1. He commits an act relating to his office but constituting an unauthorized exercise of his official functions, knowing that such act is unauthorized; or

2. He knowingly refrains from performing a duty which is imposed upon him by law or is clearly inherent in the nature of his office.

Official misconduct is a class A misdemeanor.

OTHER MISCELLANEOUS LAWS

County Law 534: County Clerk; appointments of notaries public

Each county clerk shall appoint at least one notary to notarize documents during business hours.

Such person is exempt from the examination fee and application fee (Executive Law 131).

LAWS

Banking Law 335: (Safe deposit boxes)

1.(a) If the amount due for the rental of any safe deposit box let by any lessor shall not have been paid for one year, or if the lessee thereof shall not have removed the contents thereof within thirty days from the termination of the lease therefore for any reason other than for non-payment of rent, the lessor may, at the expiration of such period, send to the lessee of such safe deposit box... a notice in writing directed to such person at his last known post-office address, notifying such lessee that if the amount due for the rental of such safe deposit box is not paid within thirty days from date, and/or if the contents thereof are not removed within thirty days from date, the lessor may, at any time thereafter, cause such safe deposit box to be opened, and the contents thereof to be inventoried and removed from such safe deposit box.

(b) At any time after expiration of thirty days from the date of mailing such notice, and the failure of the lessee of the safe deposit box to pay the amount due for the rental thereof to the date of payment, and/or remove the contents thereof, the lessor may, in the presence of a notary public and of any officer of the lessor or any other employee of the lessor designated for such purpose by the lessor, cause such safe deposit box to be opened, and the contents thereof, if any, to be removed and inventoried. .. The notary public shall file with the lessor a certificate under seal, which shall fully set out the date of the opening of such safe deposit box, the name of the lessee of such safe deposit box and a list of the contents, if any.

(c) A copy of such certificate shall within ten days after the opening be mailed by registered or certified mail, return receipt requested, to the lessee of the safe deposit box ....

HIGHLIGHTS

Banking Law 335: (Safe deposit boxes)

If a safe deposit rental fee is not paid, the lessor (bank) may give 30 days' notice to the lessee and then in the presence of a notary remove and inventory the contents.

The notary shall file with the lessor a certificate under seal stating:

1. date of opening of box

2. name of lessee

3. list of contents

A copy of this certificate must be mailed to the last known address of the lessee within 10 days of opening of safe deposit box.

LAWS

Civil Practice Law and Rules 3113: Persons before whom depositions may be taken

Depositions may be taken before any of the following persons except an attorney, or employee of an attorney, for a party or prospective party and except a person who would be disqualified to act as a juror because of interest in the event or consanguinity or affinity to a party:

1. within the state, a person authorized by the laws of the state to administer oaths....

Domestic Relations Law 11: (Marriages)

No marriage shall be valid unless solemnized by either.... (then gives a list of persons who can solemnize a marriage – which does NOT include notaries public).

OTHER RELEVANT FACTS

A member of the legislature is authorized to be appointed a notary public. (NYS Constitution, Article 3, Section 7).

A sheriff is not authorized to be appointed a notary public. (NYS Constitution, Article 13, Section 13(a)).

A notary public is not eligible to act in cases where he is financially interested in the case.

An acknowledgment so taken is a nullity with no legal effect.

A notary must officiate upon request. (PL 195). Refusal to officiate is a misdemeanor.

Perjury is giving false testimony under oath.

HIGHLIGHTS

Civil Practice Law and Rules 3113: Persons before whom depositions may be taken

In a civil proceeding, a deposition may be taken before a notary public.

Domestic Relations Law 11: (Marriages)

A notary public cannot solemnize a marriage or take the acknowledgment of parties and witnesses to a written marriage contract.

OTHER RELEVANT FACTS

A member of the legislature is authorized to be appointed a notary public. (NYS Constitution, Article 3, Section 7).

A sheriff is not authorized to be appointed a notary public. (NYS Constitution, Article 13, Section 13(a)).

A notary public is not eligible to act in cases where he is "pecuniarly interested" in the case.

An acknowledgment so taken is a nullity with no legal effect.

A notary must officiate upon request. (PL 195). Refusal to officiate is a misdemeanor.

Perjury is giving false testimony under oath.

LEGAL TERMS

The following are useful legal terms. They contain editorial comments intended to jump-start your understanding of the words. For official definitions, please consult a legal dictionary.

Acknowledgment – is a declaration that is made before an official (example: notary public) that under the person's free act and deed he did execute the instrument.

Administrator – An administrator of an estate is appointed by the court (usually Surrogate's or Supreme Court) which empowers him to manage the affairs of the decedent (dead person). The court appoints an administrator where a person dies without leaving a will, or leaves a will without naming an executor.

Affiant – An affidavit (a sworn to or affirmed written statement) is signed by a person called the affiant.

Affidavit – is a signed statement that is sworn to by the person signing it. An affidavit is sworn to in front of a notary public or other officer with authority to administer an oath.

Affirmation – A person who does not want to take an oath (because of religious, ethical or other reasons) may **affirm** as to the truthfulness of his statements. The act of affirming is called the affirmation. An affirmation is just as binding as an oath.

Apostile – An apostile is an authentication of a notarized document or county clerk certified document. It is issued by the Department of State. It is attached to the document and may be used internationally.

Attest – To attest is to be present at the execution of a written instrument and also to subscribe (sign) the written instrument as a witness to the execution of the instrument.

Attestation clause – As it refers to wills, an attestation clause is the written portion at the end of a will where the witnesses attest that the will was executed in front of them and also state the procedural manner of the execution of the will.

Authentication (notarial) – A document that is signed by a notary may be authenticated by a county clerk. The authentication is comprised of a certificate issued by the county clerk and attached to the document. The authentication verifies the notary public's authority to act as a notary public. The authentication certificate is called a "County Clerk's Certificate."

Bill of sale – A bill of sale is a written document that is given by the vendor (seller of personal property) to the vendee (buyer). It passes title from the vendor to the vendee.

Certified copy – A certified copy may NOT be issued by a notary public. They can only be issued by public officials who have custody of the original and who can certify that the copy is a true copy of the original on file.

Chattel – Chattel means property that is personal in nature, such as household goods. Chattel does NOT include real property (land, buildings).

Chattel paper – A written obligation to pay money for specific goods is known as chattel paper

Codicil – As it relates to wills, a codicil is an attachment to a will that adds to or changes (modifies) the will in some way.

Consideration – is what is given in value to induce someone to enter into a contract. Consideration examples are: property, money, services, etc.

Contempt of court – are actions which hinder the execution of court orders and display disrespect of court authority.

Contract – A contract (an agreement between parties) can be oral or written. For there to be a contract, there must be legal consideration to enter into the contract.

Conveyance – The instrument which creates, assigns, transfers or surrenders an interest in real property is called a conveyance.

Deponent – Deponent means the same as affiant. A deponent (affiant) is a person who signs the deposition and makes an oath to a written statement.

Deposition – A deposition is testimony taken before an authorized official (such as a notary public). It is taken out of court with the intention of using it at a hearing or trial.

Duress – Duress means exercising unlawful constraint on a person with the intention of forcing him to do certain acts which may be against the person's will.

Escrow – is depositing an instrument with a person who on the occurrence of an event must give the instrument to a designated person. Escrow is often used during the sale of a building.

Executor – is a person designated (named) in a will to carry out the instructions of the deceased that are listed in the will.

Ex Parte (one sided) – A court proceeding is ex parte (one sided) when it is conducted with only one of the parties being present (plaintiff or defendant).

Felony – A felony is an offense for which a sentence of imprisonment of more than a year (or death) may be imposed. Imprisonment for felonies is in a NYS prison.

Guardian – A guardian is a person in charge of another person's property or person (usually relates to guardians of minors).

Judgment – A judgment declares the rights of individuals, including that one party owes money to another and specifying the amount owed. Judgments may be final or temporary.

Jurat – A jurat is the section of an affidavit which contains the certification of the notary public that the document was sworn to in front of the notary public.

Example:
"Sworn to before me this_____day of _____, 20__"

Laches – is the negligence or delay in the assertion of a legal right. The concept of laches may be used as a defense in certain legal proceedings, such as in proceedings for unpaid rent.

Lease – Lease is a contract regarding the right to the possession of real property (land or buildings). It is made for consideration (rent, lease payments) and transfers the right to possession of real property for a period of time.

Lien – A lien is the attachment of a legal claim on property until the debt on the property is satisfied.

Litigation – is the process of pursuing a lawsuit.

Misdemeanor – A crime that is not a felony. Misdemeanors are less serious than felonies and are punishable by a sentence of imprisonment up to and including a year.

Mortgage on real property – A written instrument that is used to create a lien on real property until the debt is paid.

Notary public – is a public officer who among other things is authorized to administer oaths and affirmations relating to the truth of statements, and authorized to execute acknowledgments of deeds or writings which may thereafter be admitted into evidence.

Oath – An oath or affirmation is a verbal pledge of the truthfulness of the statements made.

An oath or affirmation must be administered as prescribed by law.

The person taking the oath must be in front of the notary. Because of this, an oath cannot be administered over the phone.

The person taking the oath must say "I do."

A corporation cannot take an oath.

A partnership cannot take an oath.

The authority of the notary public cannot be delegated to another person.

A notary public is prohibited from administering an oath to himself.

Plaintiff – A plaintiff is the party who starts a civil lawsuit.

Power of attorney – is a statement in writing by a person which gives another person the power to act for him.

Proof – as it relates to the witnessing of the execution of instruments means the formal declaration of the witness that he witnessed the execution of the instrument. The witness must state his residence and that he knew the person signing the instrument.

Protest – written statement by a notary that a promissory note or bill of exchange was presented for acceptance or payment was refused.

Seal – Notaries public are NOT required to use a seal. The only inscription required are the words, "Notary Public for the State of New York" and the name of the notary.

Signature of notary public – Notary must sign his name (same name as under which appointed). Following are required:

1. Signature and venue

2. Name (printed) beneath his signature

3. "Notary Public State of New York" beneath his signature

4. Name of county where qualified

5. Date of expiration of commission

Single woman who marries during her commission may use

1. her maiden name, OR

2. maiden name (married name)

When she renews her commission, she can:

1. renew under her maiden name, or

2. renew under her married name.

A person may be appointed under a religious name.

Statute – is a law that was created by the legislature.

Statute of frauds – A law that states that certain contracts must be in writing to be enforceable. Other contracts (if partially completed) may also be enforceable.

Statute of limitations - law which prescribe the time during which a civil action or criminal prosecution must be commenced.

Subordination clause – A clause in an agreement (contract) which allows a future mortgage to take priority over an existing mortgage.

Sunday rules for notaries public

1. An affirmation or acknowledgment MAY be taken on a Sunday.

2. A deposition in a civil proceeding CANNOT be taken on a Sunday.

Swear – any mode of oath administration that is authorized by law.

Taking an acknowledgment – includes:

1. person who is named in the instrument informing the notary that he is that person and that he indeed did execute the instrument

2. the act of the notary checking the identity of the person

The actual "taking of an acknowledgment" by the notary is noted in the notary's certification of taking the acknowledgment.

Venue – is the geographical area where the affidavit or acknowledgment is taken by notary (Example: County of Albany).

Will – the instrument in which a person sets forth his wishes relating to the disposition of his property after his death.

FEES

Total commission fee for appointment of notary public / $60.00
($20 for filing Oath of Office (which goes to county clerk) and $40
for appointment (which goes to Secretary of State)

Change of Name/Address / $10.00

Duplicate Identification Card / $10.00

Filing Certificate of Official Character / $10.00

Issuance of Certificate of Official Character / $5.00

Authentication Certificate / $3.00

Oath or Affirmation / $2.00

Acknowledgment (each person) / $2.00

Proof of Execution / $2.00

Swearing Witness / $2.00

Protest of Note, Commercial Paper, etc. / $.75

Each additional Notice of Protest (limit 5) each / $.10

QUESTIONS PRACTICE

In the following pages you will reinforce your understanding by answering two types of questions:

1. "Quick questions" (4 on a page) and
2. "Multiple Choice Questions" (2 on a page)

We suggest that you do not go on to the multiple choice questions until you have mastered the Quick Questions.

The actual test may have approximately 40 multiple choice questions.

When you think you are ready, take Practice Exam 1, then Practice Exam 2.

Whenever you answer a question incorrectly, review that section of law. Also, make sure you are confident with all the legal terms. They will form the basis of your understanding of the law.

QUICK QUESTIONS

Executive Law 130: Appointment of notaries public

T/F? A notary at the time of appointment must be either a NYS resident or have a place of business in New York State.

Executive Law 130: Appointment of notaries public

T/F? A NYS resident notary public who moves out of NYS but still maintains a place of business in NYS can continue to be a notary in NYS.

Executive Law 130: Appointment of notaries public

T/F? In certain situations, the Secretary of State is not required to satisfy himself of certain notary public requirements of an applicant, such as education.

Executive Law 130: Appointment of notaries public

T/F? The Secretary of State can remove a notary without serving a copy of the charges against him.

QUICK ANSWERS

TRUE

A notary must also be a United States citizen at time of appointment (according to statute). However, the Department of State, Division of Licensing Services web site adds that notary may also be a "permanent resident alien of the United States."

TRUE

However, if a non-resident notary ceases to have a place of business in NYS, then he vacates his office as a notary public.

TRUE

Example, when applicant applies less than 6 months after his term of notary has expired, or upon the application of an attorney admitted to practice in NYS, and certain court clerks.

FALSE

The Secretary of State must serve the charges and give him an opportunity to be heard.

QUICK QUESTIONS

Executive Law 130: Appointment of notaries public

T/F? No person shall be appointed a notary who has been convicted of any misdemeanor.

Executive Law 130: Appointment of notaries public

T/F? No person shall be appointed a notary public if he has been convicted of unlawful possession or distribution of habit forming narcotic drugs.

Executive Law 130: Appointment of notaries public

T/F? An attorney who is a notary public who moves to another state shall be deemed a resident of the county where he maintains an office in NYS.

Executive Law 131: Procedure of appointment; fees and commissions

T/F? The Secretary of State shall receive a fee of $20 for changing the name or address of a notary public.

QUICK ANSWERS

FALSE

A person cannot be appointed a notary if convicted of a FELONY.

TRUE

Also cannot be appointed a notary if convicted of vagrancy or prostitution (unless the person was subsequently pardoned or received a certificate of good conduct from a parole board).

TRUE

This section applies to attorneys who are admitted to practice in NYS and are counselors in the courts of record in New York State.

FALSE

The fee for changing the name or address of a notary public is $10. Also, the fee for issuing a duplicate I.D. (because of a lost card) is also $10.

QUICK QUESTIONS

Executive Law 132: Certificate of official character of notaries public

T/F? Only the Secretary of State may issue a Certificate of Official Character.

Executive Law 130: Appointment of notaries public

T/F? The Secretary of State shall collect $10 for the issuance of a Certificate of Official Character.

Executive Law 133: Certification of notarial signature

T/F? A certification of a notarial signature is issued by the court.

Executive Law 140:

T/F? No person removed from commissioner of deeds in New York City is eligible for reappointment as commissioner of deeds.

QUICK ANSWERS

FALSE

The county clerk may also issue a Certificate of Official Character.

TRUE

The county clerk collects $10 for the FILING of the Certificate of Official Character and $5 for the ISSUANCE of a Certificate of Official Character with seal attached.

FALSE

A certification of a notarial signature is issued by the county clerk for a fee of $3.

TRUE

Also not eligible for appointment as a notary public.

QUICK QUESTIONS

Election Law 3-200 and 3-400

T/F? A commissioner of elections or inspector of elections is not eligible for the office of notary public.

Public Officers Law 3

T/F? No person is eligible for the office of notary public who was convicted of a violation of the selective draft act of May 18, 1917.

County Law 534

T/F? There shall be at least one person in the county clerk's office who shall notarize documents for the public, free of charge.

Miscellaneous – Member of the legislature

T/F? A member of the legislature may not be appointed a notary public.

QUICK ANSWERS

FALSE

They are eligible for appointment as notary public.

TRUE

Also not eligible if convicted of a violation of the selective training and service act of 1940.

TRUE

That person shall be exempt from the notary public examination fee and application fee.

FALSE

A member of the legislature MAY be appointed a notary.

QUICK QUESTIONS

Miscellaneous – Sheriffs

T/F? A sheriff may be appointed notary public.

Notary Public – Disqualifications

T/F? A notary public shall not notarize a paper if he has a pecuniary interest in the transaction.

Executive Law 134: Signature and seal of county clerk

T/F? The signature and seal of the county clerk on a certificate of official character or authentication may be facsimile, printed or stamped.

Executive Law 135: Powers and duties

T/F? A notary shall not be liable to the parties injured for damages sustained by them as a result of the notary public's actions.

QUICK ANSWERS

FALSE

Sheriffs CANNOT hold any other office.

TRUE

Such notarization would be invalid.

TRUE

Also may be photographed or engraved thereon.

FALSE

A notary public IS liable for such damages.

QUICK QUESTIONS

Executive Law 135-a: Fraud, acting without appointment

T/F? A person not commissioned a notary public who acts as a notary public is guilty of a felony.

Executive Law 137: Statement as to authority of notaries public

T/F? A notary public who is licensed as an attorney in NYS may substitute the words "Attorney and Counselor at Law" for "Notary Public."

Executive Law 137: Statement as to authority of notaries public

T/F? No official act of a notary public shall be held invalid on account of failure to comply with the provisions listed in Executive Law 137.

Executive Law 138: Powers of notaries public

T/F? A notary public who is an employee or officer of a corporation may not take an acknowledgment of such corporation if the notary public has a financial interest in the instrument.

QUICK ANSWERS

FALSE

Such a person is guilty of a MISDEMEANOR. Also, fraud in office is also a misdemeanor (where not otherwise provided in this act.)

TRUE

Also, in NYC all notaries must affix to each instrument their official number.

TRUE

However, if such notary willfully fails to comply, he shall be subject to disciplinary action by the Secretary of State.

TRUE

Also, if the notary public is a director or agent of such corporation.

QUICK QUESTIONS

Executive Law 142-a: Validity of acts of notaries

T/F? An official certificate of a notary may be valid even if his term of office had expired.

Executive Law 142-a: Validity of acts of notaries

T/F? An official certificate of a notary may be valid even if there was an ineligibility of the notary to be appointed or commissioned.

Executive Law 142-a: Validity of acts of notaries

T/F? An official certificate of a notary may be valid even if the notary had vacated his office by changing his residence or accepting another public office.

Real Property Law 290: Definitions

T/F? The term "lien" includes every written instrument by which any estate or interest in real property is created, transferred, mortgaged or assigned.

QUICK ANSWERS

TRUE

Also valid if there is a misspelling or other error made in his appointment or commission.

TRUE

Also may be valid if there was an omission of the notary public to take or file his official oath.

TRUE

Also may be valid even if the action was taken outside the jurisdiction where the notary public was authorized to act.

FALSE

This definition applies to the legal term **"conveyance."**

QUICK QUESTIONS

Real Property Law 290: Definitions

T/F? The term "conveyance" does not include a will or a lease for a term not exceeding 3 years.

Real Property Law 298: Acknowledgments and proofs within the state

T/F? Acknowledgment or proof may be made before a justice of the peace within a county containing the town, village or city where he is authorized to perform official duties.

Real Property Law 302: Acknowledgments and proofs by married women

T/F? Acknowledgment or proof of conveyance of real estate within NYS or of any other written instrument may be made only by a married woman.

Real Property Law 304: Proof by subscribing witness

T/F? A subscribing witness must state his place of residence, but does not have to state that he knew or had satisfactory evidence of the identity of the person described in and who executed the instrument.

QUICK ANSWERS

TRUE

Also does not include an executor contract for the sale or purchase of lands.

TRUE

This applies also to town councilman, village police justice or judge of court of any inferior jurisdiction.

FALSE

It may be made by a single woman or a married woman.

FALSE

The subscribing witness MUST state that he knew the person described in and who executed the instrument or that he has satisfactory evidence that he is the same person who was a subscribing witness to the conveyance.

QUICK QUESTIONS

Real Property Law 306: Certificate of acknowledgment or proof

T/F? A person taking the acknowledgment or proof of a conveyance must endorse thereupon or attach a certificate signed by a county clerk.

Real Property Law 330: Malfeasance by officers

T/F? An officer who takes a proof of conveyance or other instrument who is guilty of malfeasance is not liable for damages to the person injured.

Real Property Law 333: When conveyances of real property not to be recorded

T/F? A conveyance of real property shall not be recorded unless it is in the English language.

Civil Practice Law and Rules 3113: Definitions

A deposition (may?/may not?) be taken before a notary public in a civil proceeding.

QUICK ANSWERS

FALSE

The certificate must be signed by the person taking the acknowledgment or proof

FALSE

He IS liable for damages to the person injured.

FALSE

MAY be recorded if there is attached to it an official translation proved and authenticated in a manner required of conveyances for recording in NYS.

A deposition MAY be taken before a notary public in a civil proceeding.

QUICK QUESTIONS

Banking Law 335: Safe deposit box

Within ___ days of the opening of the safe deposit box, a copy of the notary public's certificate must be mailed to the lessee at his last known postal address.

Domestic Relations Law 11: Marriage

A notary public (has?/does not have?) authority to solemnize marriages.

Public Officers Law 10: Official oaths

The oath of a public officer (may?/may not?) be administered by a notary public.

Judiciary Law 484: Practice by attorneys

T/F? A person can act as an attorney in New York State only if admitted to practice as an attorney or counselor in the courts of record in NYS.

QUICK ANSWERS

10 days.

Also, the box cannot be opened by the lessor until 30 days after notice to the lessee.

does NOT have

Also, a notary public may NOT take the acknowledgment of parties and witnesses to a written contract of marriage.

may

An oath to an official MAY be administered by a notary public.

TRUE

There is an exemption for the officers of societies for the prevention of cruelty and certain law students.

QUICK QUESTIONS

Judiciary Law 750: Wills

T/F? Notaries public are prohibited from executing wills because they would thereby be acting as an attorney.

Public Officers Law

T/F? A notary public is not a public officer.

Public Officers Law

A person who acts as a notary without having taken and duly filed the required oath of office is guilty of a _____.

Public Officers Law: Fees

T/F? A public officer cannot charge a fee, except where a fee or other compensation is expressly allowed by law.

QUICK ANSWERS

TRUE

Notaries public are expressly prohibited from drawing up wills.

FALSE

A notary public IS a public officer and must not act without having taken and duly filed the required oath of office.

misdemeanor

The oath must be as prescribed by law.

TRUE

Also, a public officer CANNOT charge more for the service than is allowed by law.

QUICK QUESTIONS

Public Officers Law: Fees

T/F? A public officer cannot receive a fee in advance of rendering the service.

Public Officers Law: Fees

T/F? An officer who violates the fee provisions is liable for treble damages to the person aggrieved.

Penal Law 70.00: Sentence of imprisonment for a felony

The maximum term of an indeterminate sentence shall be at least _____ years.

Penal Law 70.00: Sentence of imprisonment for a felony

For a class _____ felony, the term shall be fixed by the court and shall not exceed 7 years.

QUICK ANSWERS

FALSE

A public officer CAN receive a fee in advance IF the law allows. Also, cannot charge a fee unless the service was actually rendered by him.

TRUE

Also is liable for punishment prescribed by law for the criminal offense and removal from office.

---

3 years

The term is fixed by the judge.

"D"

Note that the maximum term of an indeterminate sentence shall be **at least** 3 years

---

QUICK QUESTIONS

Penal Law 70.15: Sentence of imprisonment for a misdemeanor

A sentence of imprisonment for a class "A" misdemeanor shall be a _____ sentence.

Penal Law 170.10: Forgery

A person is guilty of forgery in the _____ degree when he falsely makes, completes or alters a written instrument.

Penal Law 170.10: Forgery

Forgery in the second degree is a class ___ felony.

Penal Law 175.40: Issuing a false certificate

Issuing a false certificate is a class ___ felony.

QUICK ANSWERS

definite

Maximum jail for a misdemeanor is one year.

---

second

Examples: deed, will, codicil, contract, assignment, commercial instrument or public record or instrument.

"D"

This crime includes altering instruments officially issued or created by a public officer, public servant or governmental instrumentality.

"E"

A person is guilty if he issues such instrument knowing that it contains a false statement or false information.

QUICK QUESTIONS

Penal Law 195.00: Official misconduct

T/F? Official misconduct includes willfully committing an act relating to one's office constituting an unauthorized exercise of his official functions.

Penal Law 195.00: Notary officiating

T/F? An officer before whom an oath or affidavit may be taken is bound to administer the same when required.

Penal law: Perjury

A person is guilty of perjury if under oath or _____ he has given false testimony.

Definitions

An _____ is a formal declaration before an authorized officer by a person who has executed an instrument that such execution is his act and deed.

QUICK ANSWERS

TRUE

Also includes refraining from performing a duty which is imposed upon him by law or is clearly inherent in the nature of his office.

TRUE

Refusal to do so is a misdemeanor.

affirmation

The testimony must have been given on a material matter.

acknowledgment

The officer must know that the person making it is the person described and who executed the instrument.

QUICK QUESTIONS

Acknowledgments

T/F? It is not essential that the person who executed the instrument sign his name in the presence of the notary.

Acknowledgment

A notary who takes an acknowledgment over the telephone is guilty of a _____.

Acknowledgment

Unless the person who makes the acknowledgment appears in front of the notary, the notary's certificate that he so came is _____.

Certificates of acknowledgment

Making a false certificate is forgery in the _____ degree.

<u>QUICK ANSWERS</u>

TRUE

However, taking acknowledgments over the phone is illegal.

---

misdemeanor

However, it is not essential that the person sign in front of the notary.

---

fraudulent

However, it is not essential that the person who executed the instrument sign his name in the presence of the notary.

---

second

This is punishable by a term not exceeding 7 years.

QUICK QUESTIONS

Acknowledgment

A notary public (should?/should not?) take an acknowledgment to a legal instrument to which the notary is a party in interest.

Definitions

An (administrator?/affiant?) is a person appointed by the court to manage the estate of a deceased person who left no will.

Definitions

A (statute?/affidavit?) is a signed statement, duly sworn, before a notary public or other officer authorized to administer oaths.

Definitions

An (attestation?/apostile?) is a Department of State authentication attached to a notarized and county-certified document for international use.

QUICK ANSWERS

should not

A notary is liable for damages sustained due to a false certificate.

---

administrator

An affiant is a person who makes and subscribes his signature to an affidavit.

---

affidavit

A statute is a law established by an act of the legislature.

---

apostile

To attest is to witness the execution of a written instrument, at the request of the person who makes it, and subscribe the same as witness.

QUICK QUESTIONS

Definitions

An (authentication?/affirmation?) is a certificate attached by a county clerk to a certificate of proof or acknowledgment or oath signed by a notary.

Definitions

In an _____ _____ the witnesses certify that the instrument has been executed before them, and the manner of the execution of the same.

Definitions

An _____ is a solemn declaration made by persons who conscientiously decline taking an oath.

Definitions

A ___ __ ___ is a written instrument given to pass title of personal property from vendor to vendee.

QUICK ANSWERS

authentication

This county clerk's certificate authenticates or verifies the authority of the notary public to act as such.

attestation clause

Example: an attestation clause found at the end of a will.

affirmation

It is equivalent to an oath and just as binding.

bill of sale

Personal property, such as household goods and fixtures, is known as "chattel."

QUICK QUESTIONS

Definitions

_____ _____ is a writing or writings which evidence both an obligation to pay money and a security interest in specific goods.

Definitions

A _____ is an instrument made subsequent to a will and attached to the will.

Definitions

_____ is anything of value given to induce someone to enter into a contract.

Definitions

A _____ _____ is a copy of a public record signed and certified as a true copy by the public official having custody of the original.

<u>QUICK ANSWERS</u>

chattel paper

The agreement which creates or provides for the security interest is known as a security agreement.

codicil

The codicil adds to or modifies the will in some respects.

consideration

Consideration may be money, personal services, or even love and affection.

certified copy

A notary has NO authority to issue certified copies.

QUICK QUESTIONS

Definitions

Behavior that is disrespectful of the authority of a court which disrupts the execution of court orders is known as

_____ __ _____.

Definitions

A _____ is an agreement between competent parties to do or not do certain things for legal consideration.

Definitions

Generally, every instrument (except a will) by which any estate or interest in real property is created, transferred, assigned or surrendered is known as a _____.

Definitions

Another term for "County Clerk's Certificate" is _____.

QUICK ANSWERS

contempt of court

Contempt of court can be punished by the court.

contract

A contract can be written or oral.

conveyance

The instrument must be in writing.

authentication

Authentication (notarial).

QUICK QUESTIONS

Definitions

A _____ is one who makes an oath to a written statement.

Definitions

A _____ is the testimony of a witness taken out of court, before a notary or other person.

Definitions

Constraint exercised upon a person whereby he is forced to do some act against his will is known as _____.

Definitions

_____ is the placing of an instrument in the hands of a person as a depository who on the happening of an event must deliver it to a third person.

QUICK ANSWERS

deponent

A "deponent" is also known as an "affiant."

deposition

A deposition is intended to be used at the time of trial or hearing.

duress

The "constraint" must be "unlawful constraint."

escrow

The agreement should be unalterable.

QUICK QUESTIONS

Definitions

An _____ is one named in a will to carry out the provisions of the will.

Definitions

___ ____ means to do a hearing or examination in the presence of, or on papers filed by, one party in the absence of the other.

Definitions

A ____ is a crime punishable by death or imprisonment over one year.

Definitions

A ____ is a person in charge of a minor's person.

QUICK ANSWERS

executor

A will specifies the disposition of one's property to take effect after death.

ex parte

Ex parte means 'from one side only.'

felony

The imprisonment for a felony is in a state prison.

guardian

A guardian may also be in charge of a minor's property.

QUICK QUESTIONS

Definitions

A _____ is a decree of a court declaring that one party is indebted to another and fixing the amount of such indebtedness.

Executive Law 130: Appointment of notaries public

The _____ appoints and commissions notaries public in New York State.

Executive Law 130: Appointment of notaries public

The jurisdiction of notaries public is _____.

Executive Law 130: Appointment of notaries public

Notaries public are appointed for _____ years.

QUICK ANSWERS

judgment

A judgment can be for money or can determine the rights of parties.

Secretary of State

The Secretary of State appoints notaries for a 4 year term.

New York State (statewide)

(Notaries are appointed by the Secretary of State.)

4 years

At the end of that period they may apply to renew their term (reappointment).

QUICK QUESTIONS

Executive Law 130: Appointment of notaries public

Applications for notaries public are as prescribed by _____.

Executive Law 130: Appointment of notaries public

Attorneys and _____ are exempt from taking the notary public exam.

Executive Law 130: Appointment of notaries public

Applicants for notary public must have the equivalent of a _____ school education.

Executive Law 130: Appointment of notaries public

The _____ may suspend or remove a notary public from office.

QUICK ANSWERS

the Secretary of State

(The term of a notary public is 4 years.)

certain court clerks

(that work for the NYS Unified Court System and have been appointed as a result of a civil service exam in the Court Clerk series of exams.)

common school

Applicants must also be U.S. citizens at the time of appointment, as per Executive Law 130 (case law may differ).

Secretary of State

Grounds for removal include misconduct and fraud.

QUICK QUESTIONS

Executive Law 130: Appointment of notaries public

A person convicted of a _____ cannot be appointed a notary public.

Executive Law 130: Appointment of notaries public

A person convicted of unlawfully possessing or distributing habit forming narcotic drugs (can?/cannot?) be appointed a notary public.

Executive Law 130: Appointment of notaries public

T/F? A person sought to be removed as a notary public must be served a copy of the charges.

Executive Law 131: Procedure for appointment, fees and commissions

An oath of _____ shall be submitted to the Secretary of State with the application for notary public.

QUICK ANSWERS

felony

(A person convicted of a misdemeanor may be appointed.)

cannot

Also cannot be appointed if convicted of unlawful entry of a building or aiding escape from prison.

TRUE

The person must also be given an opportunity to be heard.

office

Also, the oath must be duly executed before a person authorized to administer an oath.

QUICK QUESTIONS

Executive Law 131: Procedure for appointment, fees and commissions

The fee for notary public appointment is _____.

Executive Law 131: Procedure for appointment, fees and commissions

The notary public identification card contains the appointee's name, address, county and _____.

Executive Law 131: Procedure for appointment, fees and commissions

The Secretary of State must send $20 fee (apportioned from the $60 fee) to the _____ by the 10th day of the following month.

Executive Law 131: Procedure for appointment, fees and commissions (Application for reappointment)

The _____ makes an index of commissions and official signatures transmitted by the county clerk.

QUICK ANSWERS

$60

($20 of this amount is transmitted to the county clerk.)

commission term

(The commission term is for 4 years.)

county clerk

(Must also send a certified copy of the oath of office.)

Secretary of State

QUICK QUESTIONS

Executive Law 131: Procedure for appointment, fees and commissions (Reappointment)

The _____ issues reappointment commissions to notaries public.

Executive Law 131: Procedure for appointment, fees and commissions

The _____ shall receive a fee of $60 from each applicant for reappointment.

Executive Law 131: Procedure for appointment, fees and commissions

The county clerk shall transmit to the Secretary of State _____ from the fee for reappointment.

Executive Law 131: Procedure for appointment, fees and commissions

Generally, the Secretary of State shall receive a non-refundable fee of ___ for changing the name or address of a notary.

QUICK ANSWERS

county clerk

After issuing the commissions, the county clerk sends the list of commissions to the Secretary of State

county clerk

(Along with the $60 fee there must also be submitted by the notary public a reappointment application.)

$40

The fee must be submitted by the 10th of the following month.

$10

(Note that changes made in an application for reappointment do not require this fee.)

QUICK QUESTIONS

Executive Law 131: Procedure for appointment, fees and commissions

The Secretary of State may issue a duplicate identification card for a fee of ___.

Executive Law 132: Certificates of official character of notaries public

The county clerk where the notary commission is filed or the _____ may certify as to the official character of such notary public.

Executive Law 132: Certificates of official character of notaries public

The Secretary of State shall collect for a certificate of official character ISSUED by him the sum of $___.

Executive Law 132: Certificates of official character of notaries public

The county clerk charges a fee of $___ to FILE a certificate of official character.

QUICK ANSWERS

$10

(Each duplicate card must have stamped across its face the word "duplicate" and must have bear the same number as the one it replaces.)

Secretary of State

A notary public may file his autograph signature and a certificate of official character in the office of any county clerk in New York State.

$10

Also, the Secretary of State shall collect for a certificate of official character FILED by him the sum of $ $10.

$10

The county clerk charges a fee of $10 to FILE a certificate of official character (and $5 to ISSUE a certificate of official character).

QUICK QUESTIONS

Executive Law 132: Certificates of official character of notaries public

For each certificate of official character issued by a county clerk, a fee of $____ shall be collected by the county clerk.

Executive Law 140

A person removed from office as commissioner of deeds (is?/is not?) eligible to be appointed a notary public.

Executive Law 140

Acting as commissioner of deeds after removal is a ____ offense.

Election Law 3-200 and 3-400

A commissioner of elections (is?/is not/) eligible for the office of notary public.

QUICK ANSWERS

$5

For each certificate of official character ISSUED by a county clerk, a fee of $5 shall be collected by the county clerk.

IS NOT

Also, cannot be reappointed commissioner of deeds.

misdemeanor

(A misdemeanor offense is punishable with prison up to and including one year.)

IS

Also, an inspector of elections is eligible for the office of notary public.

QUICK QUESTIONS

Public Officers Law 3

A person convicted of a violation of the selective draft act of the U.S. (is?/is not/) eligible for appointment as notary public.

County Law 534

Each county clerk shall designate ay least ____ of his staff to act as notary public to notarize documents during business hours at no charge.

NYS Constitution, Article 13, Section 13(a)

A sheriff (may/?may not?) hold another office.

NYS Constitution, Article 3, Section 7

A member of the legislature (may?/may not?) be appointed a notary public.

QUICK ANSWERS

IS NOT

Also not eligible if convicted of violating amendments to the selective draft act.

one

The individual shall be exempt from the examination fee and the application fee.

MAY NOT

However, a member of the legislature MAY be a notary public.

MAY

A sheriff may not be appointed a notary public.

QUICK QUESTIONS

Case Law

A notary public who is pecuniarly interested in a transaction (is?/is not?) capable of acting as a notary public in that case.

Executive Law 134

T/F? The signature and seal of a county clerk on a certificate of authentication may be facsimile or printed.

Executive Law 135

T/F? Notaries public are empowered to administer oaths and affirmations.

Executive Law 135

T/F? Notaries cannot take affidavits and depositions.

QUICK ANSWERS

IS NOT

Also cannot do so if the notary is a party to the transaction.

TRUE

Signature may also be stamped, photographed or engraved.

TRUE

They are also empowered to take affidavits and depositions.

FALSE

They can also certify acknowledgments and proofs of deeds, mortgages and powers of attorney and other instruments.

QUICK QUESTIONS

Executive Law 135

T/F? Notaries can receive and certify acknowledgments or proofs of deeds, mortgages and powers of attorney and other instruments.

Executive Law 135

T/F? Notaries cannot demand acceptance or payment of foreign and inland bills of exchange.

Executive Law 135

T/F? Notaries can exercise powers and duties as by the laws of nations and according to commercial usage.

Executive Law 135

T/F? A notary who is an attorney may administer an oath or affirmation to his client in respect of any matter, claim, action or proceeding.

<u>QUICK ANSWERS</u>

TRUE

Notaries can also administer oaths and affirmations.

FALSE

Also, a notary can demand payment of promissory notes and obligations in writing.

TRUE

Notaries can exercise powers and duties as by the laws of nations and according to commercial usage or by the laws of any other government or country, provided that when exercising such powers the notary shall set forth the name of such other jurisdiction.

TRUE

Attorney must be admitted to practice in New York State.

QUICK QUESTIONS

Executive Law 135

T/F? A notary is not liable to parties injured for damages sustained by them.

Executive Law 135-a

A person who acts as a notary without first being appointed a notary is guilty of a _____.

Executive Law 135-a

A notary who practices fraud or deceit is guilty of a _____ offense.

Executive Law 136

A notary public is entitled to a fee of $____ for administering an oath or affirmation.

QUICK ANSWERS

FALSE

The notary IS liable for damages resulting from his misconduct.

misdemeanor

A misdemeanor is punishable with a jail term of up to and including a year.

misdemeanor

The notary is also liable for damages to the other parties.

$2

The fee may be different only when otherwise prescribed by law.

QUICK QUESTIONS

Executive Law 136

The fee for taking and certifying an acknowledgment or proof of execution of a written instrument is $_____.

Executive Law 142-a

T/F? An act or certificate of a notary is not made invalid due to the ineligibility of the notary public or commissioner of deeds to be appointed or commissioned.

Executive Law 142-a

T/F? An act or certificate of a notary is made invalid by a misnomer or misspelling of his name or other error made in his appointment or commission.

Executive Law 142-a

T/F? An act or certificate of a notary is made invalid by the expiration of the notary public's term, commission or appointment.

QUICK ANSWERS

$2

(for each person)

TRUE

There are exceptions, including where a person knew of the defect.

FALSE

Also NOT invalid if due to the expiration of his term.

FALSE

Also not invalid if due to misnomer or misspelling of name or other error made in his appointment or commission.

QUICK QUESTIONS

Executive Law 142-a

T/F? An act or certificate of a notary is not made invalid by the notary vacating his office by change of his residence, or by acceptance of another public office.

Executive Law 142-a

T/F? An act or certificate of a notary is not made invalid by the fact that the action was taken outside the jurisdiction where the notary public was authorized to act.

Real Property Law 298

T/F? The acknowledgment or proof WITHIN THE STATE of a conveyance of real property situated in NYS may be made at any place WITHIN THE STATE before a notary public, a justice of the supreme court, an official referee or an official examiner of title.

Real Property Law 298 T/F? The acknowledgment or proof WITHIN A DISTRICT may be made where any of the following officers are authorized to perform official duties: a judge of any court of record, commissioner of deeds, mayor or recorder of a city, a surrogate, county judge or the county clerk or other recording officer of a county.

QUICK ANSWERS

TRUE

and generally by any other action on his part.

TRUE

Same applies to commissioner of deeds.

TRUE

Note that the subject area is WITHIN THE STATE.

TRUE

Note that the subject area is WITHIN THE DISTRICT.

QUICK QUESTIONS

Real Property Law 298 T/F?

The acknowledgment or proof WITHIN A COUNTY may be made where any of the following officers are authorized to perform official duties: justice of peace, town councilman, village police justice, or a judge of any court of inferior local jurisdiction.

Real Property Law 302

The acknowledgment of a conveyance of real property within the state may be made by a married woman or _____ woman.

Real Property Law 303

T/F? An officer may take an acknowledgment even if he has no satisfactory evidence that the person making it is the person described in and who executed such instrument.

Real Property Law 304

When the execution of a conveyance is proved by a subscribing witness, such witness must state his _____ and that he knew the person described in and who executed the conveyance.

QUICK ANSWERS

TRUE

Note that the subject area is WITHIN A COUNTY.

unmarried

Married and unmarried women have the same rights.

FALSE

The officer MUST satisfy himself as to the identity of the person.

place of residence

and if the place of residence is in a city, must state his street and street number.

QUICK QUESTIONS

Real Property Law 333

T/F? Generally, for a record to be recorded it must be in the _____ language.

Real Property Law 333

T/F? If a record to be recorded is not in the English language, it must have attached a translation duly executed and acknowledged.

Banking Law 335

When a safe deposit box is opened as per this section, the notary public shall file with the lessor a certificate under seal which states the _____ of the safe deposit box and the name of the lessee.

Civil Practice Law and Rules 3113

T/F? In a civil proceeding a deposition may be taken before a notary public.

QUICK ANSWERS

English

Proper names may be in another language, but must be written in English characters.

TRUE

The translation must be by a person duly designated for such purpose by the county judge of the county where conveyance is to be recorded, or a justice of the supreme court.

date of opening

The certificate must also contain a list of the contents of the safe deposit box.

TRUE

Example: examination before trial (EBT)

QUICK QUESTIONS

Domestic Relations Law

T/F? A notary may solemnize a marriage.

Domestic Relations Law

A notary (may?/may not?) take the acknowledgment of parties and witnesses to a written contract of marriage.

Public Officers Law 10

T/F? A notary may administer an oath to a public officer.

Public Officers Law 750

A notary (may?/may not?) prepare a will.

QUICK ANSWERS

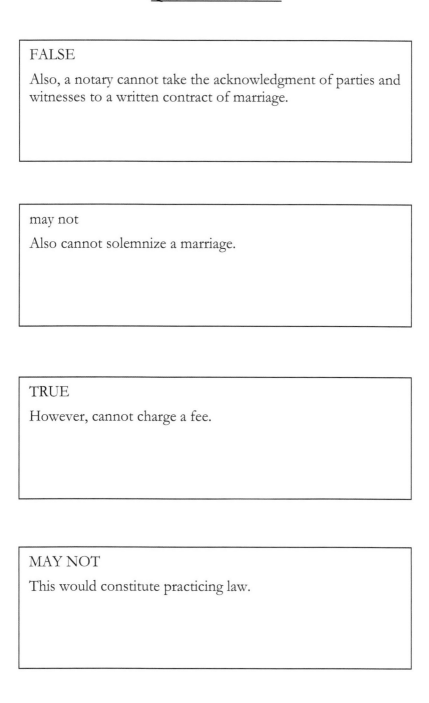

FALSE

Also, a notary cannot take the acknowledgment of parties and witnesses to a written contract of marriage.

may not

Also cannot solemnize a marriage.

TRUE

However, cannot charge a fee.

MAY NOT

This would constitute practicing law.

QUICK QUESTIONS

Public Officers Law 69

A notary (is entitled?/is not entitled?) to a fee for administering the oath of office to a member of the legislature, to any military office, to an inspector, or clerk of the poll.

Executive Law 135-a

T/F? A notary may be removed from office for making a misstatement of a material fact in his application for appointment.

Public Officers Law 15

T/F? A notary public is a public officer.

Penal Law 195

If a notary refrains from performing a duty imposed on him by law, he is guilty of official _____.

QUICK ANSWERS

IS NOT ENTITLED

Also not entitled to a fee for administering an oath to any other public officer or public employee.

TRUE

Also may be removed for misconduct and fraud.

TRUE

Because of this, a notary shall not execute any of the functions of his office without prior having taken and filed the required oath of office.

misconduct

Official misconduct is a class "A" misdemeanor.

MULTIPLE CHOICE QUESTIONS

Who commissions notaries public?

A. State Comptroller

B. County Clerks

C. Attorney General

D. Secretary of State

The application fee for a notary public commission is:

A. $40

B. $60

C. $80

D. $90

MULTIPLE CHOICE ANSWERS

D. Secretary of State

(Executive Law 130)

A record of the commissions is kept by the county clerk.

B. $60

(Schedule of Fees; Executive Law 130)

The Secretary of State keeps $40 and sends $20 to the county clerk where the appointee resides.

The county clerk makes an index of the commissions and official signatures transmitted to the county clerk by the Secretary of State.

MULTIPLE CHOICE QUESTIONS

An application for a notary public commission must be submitted to:

A. County Clerk.

B. Local civil court.

C. Division of Licensing Services.

D. None of the above.

Which of the following is correct?
An application for a notary public commission must include:

A. $45 filing fee.

B. a photograph of the applicant.

C. a copy of the applicant's social security card.

D. oath of office which must be sworn and notarized.

MULTIPLE CHOICE ANSWERS

C. Division of Licensing Services

(Executive Law 131)

The commission itself is issued by the Secretary of State

D. oath of office which must be sworn and notarized

(Executive Law 131)

The filing fee is $60, and NO copy of a social security card or photograph is required.

MULTIPLE CHOICE QUESTIONS

A "pass slip" showing that the applicant passed the notary public exam must be submitted along with:

A. application for citizenship.

B. application for a notary public commission.

C. application for a non driver state I.D.

D. None of the above.

Notary public examinations are regularly scheduled:

A. throughout NYS.

B. in NYC and Albany only.

C. only in counties with a population of over 1,000,000.

D. None of the above

MULTIPLE CHOICE ANSWERS

B. application for a notary public commission

(Division of licensing services booklet)

An applicant for a notary commission must submit to the Secretary of State:

1. $60 fee

2. application (includes oath of office)

A. throughout NYS

(Division of Licensing Services Booklet)

Also, notaries public are commissioned in their county of residence.

MULTIPLE CHOICE QUESTIONS

An individual who is an attorney:

A. cannot be a notary public.

B. can be a notary public if admitted to practice in NYS.

C. must be a notary public in all cases.

D. None of the above

The term of a commission of a notary public is _____.

A. 2 years

B. 4 years

C. 5 years

D. 6 years

MULTIPLE CHOICE ANSWERS

B. can be a notary public if admitted to practice in NYS.

(Executive Law 130)

Even if the attorney moves out of NYS, he can continue to act as a notary if he has a place of business within NYS.

B. 4 years

(Executive Law 130)

At the end of his term, a notary public can apply for reappointment.

MULTIPLE CHOICE QUESTIONS

Where are notaries public commissioned?

A. in their county of birth

B. in their city of preference

C. in their county of residence

D. None of the above

Which of the following is not correct?

After the Secretary of State approves an applicant for a notary public commission, he forwards the following to the appropriate county clerk:

A. the original oath of office

B. the signature of the notary public

C. the original social security card of the applicant

D. the notary public commission

MULTIPLE CHOICE ANSWERS

C. in their county of residence

(Executive Law 131)

If the notary does not reside in NYS, but has a place of business in NYS, then the county where he does business is considered his county of residence.

C. the original social security card of the applicant

(Executive Law 131)

The county clerk keeps an index of the commissions and official signatures sent to the county clerk by the Secretary of State.

MULTIPLE CHOICE QUESTIONS

Who maintains a record of the notaries public commissions and signatures?

A. the city comptroller

B. the county clerk

C. the Chief Clerk of the Supreme Court

D. None of the above

The public may obtain a certification of the notarial signature at the:

A. mayor's office

B. office of the attorney general

C. county clerk's office

D. None of the above

MULTIPLE CHOICE ANSWERS

B. the county clerk

(Executive Law 131)

The county clerk makes this index upon receipt of required information from the Secretary of State, and a $20 fee, by the 10th day of the following month.

C. county clerk's office

(Executive Law 131)

The fee for a certification of a notarial signature is $3.

MULTIPLE CHOICE QUESTIONS

If a non-resident attorney or person becomes a notary, the oath of office and signature must be filed in the office of the county clerk of the county where:

A. the attorney passed his bar exam.

B. the person or attorney live.

C. the office or place of business is located in NYS.

D. None of the above.

Acknowledgments and affidavits:

A. may not be taken over the phone.

B. may be taken over the phone if the affiant is ill.

C. may be taken over the phone if the affiant is a non-resident.

D. None of the above

MULTIPLE CHOICE ANSWERS

C. the office or place of business is located in NYS

(Division of Licensing Services Booklet)

Non-residents of NYS who are notaries are considered (deemed) to be residents of the county where their office or place of business is located.

A. may not be taken over the phone.

(Division of Licensing Services Booklet and case law)

In the Matter of Napolis, 169 App. Div. 469, 472, the court condemned the "acts of notaries taking acknowledgments or affidavits without the presence of the party whose acknowledgment is taken for the affiant."

MULTIPLE CHOICE QUESTIONS

Which of the following may be used when a person conscientiously declines to take an oath?

1. "Do you solemnly swear that the contents of this affidavit subscribed by you is correct and true?"

2. "Do you solemnly, sincerely and truly declare and affirm that the statements made by you are true and correct?"

A. 1 only is correct.

B. Both 1 and 2 are correct.

C. 2 only is correct.

D. Neither 1 nor 2 are correct.

Which of the following 4 statements is false? A notary public:

A. may not give advice on the law.

B. may not ask for and get legal business to refer to a lawyer with whom he has business or receives consideration for sending the business.

C. may agree to divide his fees with a lawyer.

D. may not advertise that he has powers not given to the notary by the laws under which the attorney was appointed.

MULTIPLE CHOICE ANSWERS

C. 2 only is correct.

(Division of Licensing Services Booklet and case law)

The statement must be made in front of an officer authorized to administer it.

C. May agree to divide his fees with a lawyer.

(Division of Licensing Services Booklet)

Making such an agreement would constitute practicing law, something which notaries are expressly prohibited from doing.

<u>MULTIPLE CHOICE QUESTIONS</u>

The jurisdiction of notaries public is:

A. the county of residence only.

B. the county of place of business only.

C. the city of residence or place of business only.

D. co-extensive with the boundaries of New York State.

Which of the following is false?
For a person to be appointed a notary public he must be:

A. a citizen of the United States

B. a resident of NYS or have a place of business in NYS.

C. a foreign national.

D, not convicted of a felony.

MULTIPLE CHOICE ANSWERS

D. co-extensive with the boundaries of New York State.

(Executive Law 130)

The jurisdiction of notaries appointed in any county in New York State is statewide.

C. a foreign national.

(Executive Law 130)

However, a person (US citizen) may reside out of NYS if he maintains an office in NYS.

MULTIPLE CHOICE QUESTIONS

Which of the following appears on a notary public identification card?

1. appointee's name and address

2. county and commission term

A. 1 only.

B. 2 only.

C. Both 1 and 2.

D. Neither 1 nor 2.

The commission and a certified copy or original oath of office and official signature, and $____ from the application fee shall be sent by the Secretary of State to the county clerk where the appointee resides by the ____ day of the following month.

A. $20....20th

B. $10....10th

C. $10....20th

D. $20....10th

MULTIPLE CHOICE ANSWERS

C. Both 1 and 2.

(Executive Law 131)

The I.D. card is sent to the appointee, and the commission and certified copy of the original oath of office and original signature and $20 is transmitted by the Secretary of State to the county clerk of the county of appointee's residence.

D. $20....10th

(Executive Law 131)

The Secretary of State retains $40 of the $60 application fee.

MULTIPLE CHOICE QUESTIONS

The county clerk collects a non-refundable application fee of $___ from each applicant for REAPPOINTMENT.

A. $20

B. $40

C. $60

D. $80

Except for changes made in a notary public's application for reappointment, the Secretary of State shall receive a fee of $____ for changing the name or address of the notary.

A. $10

B. $20

C. $30

D. $40

MULTIPLE CHOICE ANSWERS

C. $60

(Executive Law 131)

The county clerk then sends $40 of the $60 fee to the Secretary of State.

A. $10

(Executive Law 131)

The fee for issuing a duplicate I.D. card is also $10

MULTIPLE CHOICE QUESTIONS

The Secretary of State may issue a duplicate I.D. card to a notary to replace one that was lost, destroyed or damaged upon the payment of a fee of $___.

A. $60

B. $40

C. $20

D. $10

When the Secretary of State issues a certificate of official character, he must collect a fee of $___.

A. $5

B. $10

C. $20

D. $30

MULTIPLE CHOICE ANSWERS

D. $10

(Executive Law 131)

Each duplicate I.D. card must have the word "duplicate" stamped on it.

B. $10

(Executive Law 132)

The certificate of official character may also be ISSUED by the appropriate county clerk. The fee is $5.

(For FILING a certificate of official character with the county clerk, the fee is $10.)

MULTIPLE CHOICE QUESTIONS

For each certificate of official character issued by a county clerk, the sum of $____ shall be collected.

A. $5

B. $10

C. $20

D. $30

The fee for a certification of a notarial signature issued by a county clerk is $____.

A. $2

B. $3

C. $6

D. $10

MULTIPLE CHOICE ANSWERS

A. $5

(Executive Law 132)

Fee for the FILING with the county clerk of a certificate of official character is $10.

Fee for the ISSUANCE by the county clerk of a certificate of official character is $5.

B. $3

(Executive Law 133)

The certificate of authentication entitles the instrument to be read into evidence or recorded in any instance where a certificate is necessary for those purposes.

MULTIPLE CHOICE QUESTIONS

If a person who was removed from the office of commissioner of deeds (NYC) executes an instrument while posing as a commissioner of deeds, he shall be guilty of _____.

A. a violation

B. a felony

C. a misdemeanor

D. a petty offense

Which of the following two choices are correct?

The following persons are eligible for the office of notary public:

    1. a commissioner of elections

    2. an inspector of elections

A. Choice 1 only is correct.

B. Choice 2 only is correct.

C. Both choices 1 and 2 are correct.

D. Neither choice 1 nor choice 2 are correct.

MULTIPLE CHOICE ANSWERS

C. a misdemeanor

(Executive Law 140)

The same applies where the person poses as a notary.

C. Both choices 1 and 2 are correct.

(Election Law 3-200 and 3-400)

Also, a member of the legislature IS eligible.

A sheriff is NOT eligible.

MULTIPLE CHOICE QUESTIONS

Each county clerk must designate at least _____ employee(s) from his office to act as a notary public and notarize documents for the public for free.

A. one

B. two

C. three

D. four

Which of the following are eligible to be appointed notaries public?

1. a member of the legislature

2. a sheriff

A. 1 only is eligible for appointment.

B. 2 only is eligible for appointment.

C. Both 1 and 2 are eligible for appointment.

D. Neither 1 nor 2 are eligible for appointment.

MULTIPLE CHOICE ANSWERS

A. one

(County Law 534)

The individual(s) so appointed by the county clerk are exempt from paying the notary public application fee and notary public examination fee.

A. 1 only is eligible for appointment

(NYS Constitution, Article 3, Section 7 and

Article 13, Section 13(a))

Sheriffs are prohibited from holding any other office.

MULTIPLE CHOICE QUESTIONS

Which of the following are correct?

1. A notary public may be disqualified to act if he has an interest in the case.

2. A notary public interested in a conveyance is not competent to take the acknowledgment of an instrument.

A. 1 only is correct.

B. 2 only is correct.

C. Both 1 and 2 are correct.

D. Neither 1 nor 2 are correct.

Generally, a notary is entitled to a fee of $___ for administering an oath or affirmation and certifying the same when required.

A. $2

B. $4

C. $5

D. $6

MULTIPLE CHOICE ANSWERS

C. Both 1 and 2 are correct.

(Division of Licensing Services Booklet)

Generally, if a notary has a money interest in a case, then he is disqualified from acting as a notary in that case.

A. $2

(Executive Law 136)

The fee is $2 unless otherwise specifically prescribed by statute.

MULTIPLE CHOICE QUESTIONS

Generally, a notary is entitled to $____ for taking and certifying the acknowledgment or proof of execution of a written instrument (by one person). He is also entitled to $____ for each additional person and also $____ for swearing a witness thereto.

A. $2, $4, $6

B. $2, $2, $2

C. $4, $4, $4

D. None of the above.

A notary public who is duly licensed as an attorney and counselor at law in NYS may in his discretion substitute the following for the words "Notary Public."

A. Commissioner of NYS

B. Qualified Commissioner

C. Counselor at Law

D. None of the above

MULTIPLE CHOICE ANSWERS

B. $2, $2, $2

(Executive Law 136)

List of $2 fees:

Oath or affirmation / $2

Acknowledgment / $2 for each person

Swearing a witness / $ 2

Proof of execution / $2 (each person)

C. Counselor at Law

(Executive Law 137)

The attorney must be duly licensed as an attorney and counselor at law in New York State.

MULTIPLE CHOICE QUESTIONS

Which of the following is the best answer?

Section 142-a of the Executive Law states that an act of a notary or commissioner of deeds is valid even if:

A. the notary was not eligible to be appointed.

B. there existed a misspelling or other error made in the appointment of the notary.

C. the term of the notary had expired.

D. All of the above are correct.

Which of the following three choices are correct?

The term "conveyance" includes:

1. a written instrument by which an estate in real property is created.

2. a written instrument which effects title to real property.

3. a will.

A. 1 only is correct.

B. 1 and 2 only are correct.

C. 1, 2 and 3 are all correct.

D. 2 only is correct.

MULTIPLE CHOICE ANSWERS

D. All of the above are correct.

(Executive Law 142-a)

Also valid if notary had vacated his office because of a change in his residence, or if the notary acted outside the jurisdiction where he was authorized to act.

B. 1 and 2 only are correct.

(Real Property Law 290)

"Conveyance" also includes a written instrument by which an estate in real property is transferred, assigned or mortgaged.

MULTIPLE CHOICE QUESTIONS

The acknowledgment or proof within NYS of a conveyance of real property in NYS may be made AT ANY PLACE WITHIN THE STATE, before:

1. a justice of the supreme court

2. an official examiner of title or an official referee

3. a notary public

A. Only 1 and 3 are correct.

B. Only 2 and 3 are correct.

C. 1, 2 and 3 are all correct.

D. Only 3 is correct.

The acknowledgment or proof, within the state, of a conveyance of real property in NYS may be made WITHIN THE DISTRICT where the officer is authorized before:

1. the mayor or recorder of a city

2. commissioner of deeds, judge or clerk of any court of record

3. county clerk or other recording officer of the county.

A. 1, 2 and 3 are correct.

B. Only 1 and 2 are correct.

C. Only 2 and 3 are correct.

D. Only 3 is correct.

MULTIPLE CHOICE ANSWERS

C. 1, 2 and 3 are all correct.

(Property Law 298)

Note the difference between the choices in this question and the choices in the following question. The difference is in the GEOGRAPHICAL AREA OF NYS where the acknowledgment may be made. The jurisdiction of the listed officials is different. It varies from statewide to local.

A. 1, 2 and 3 are correct.

(Property Law 298)

Note the difference between the choices in this question and the choices in the previous question. The difference is in the GEOGRAPHICAL AREA OF NYS where the acknowledgment may be made. The jurisdiction of the listed officials is different. It varies from statewide to local.

MULTIPLE CHOICE QUESTIONS

Which of the following fees is not correct?

A. Appointment as Notary Public fee (total) / $60

B. Change of Name/Address / $20

C. Duplicate Identification Card / $10

D. Issuance of Certificate of Official Character / $5

Which of the following fees is not correct?

A. Filing Certificate of Official Character / $10

B. Authentication Certificate / $3

C. Protest of Note, Commercial Paper, etc. / $.75

D. Oath or Affirmation / $4

MULTIPLE CHOICE ANSWERS

B. Change of Name/Address / $20

(Schedule of Fees)

The correct fee for Change of Name/Address is $10

D. Oath or Affirmation / $4

(Schedule of Fees)

The correct fee for Oath or Affirmation is $2

MULTIPLE CHOICE QUESTIONS

Which of the following fees is not correct?

A. Acknowledgment (each person) / $2

B. Proof of Execution (each person) / $2

C. Swearing Witness / $2

D. Duplicate Identification Card / $20

A declaration before a duly authorized officer by a person who has executed an instrument that the execution is his act is known as _____.

A. a conveyance

B. a jurat

C. an affiant

D. an acknowledgment

MULTIPLE CHOICE ANSWERS

D. Duplicate Identification Card / $20

(Schedule of Fees)

The fee for a duplicate identification card is / $10

D. an acknowledgment

(Definitions)

The term acknowledgment is also used to mean the certificate of an officer who is authorized to take an acknowledgment of the conveyance of real property.

MULTIPLE CHOICE QUESTIONS

Someone appointed by a court to manage the affairs (estate) of a person who died without a will is known as _____.

A. a plaintiff

B. an affiant

C. an administrator

D. an executor

A person who signs an affidavit is called _____.

A. an administrator

B. an affiant

C. a jurat

D. an executor

MULTIPLE CHOICE ANSWERS

C. an administrator

(Definitions)

If the person dies with a will and names in the will the person to manage his affairs, then that person is called the executor.

B. an affiant

(Definitions)

The affiant can either affirm or swear (take an oath).

MULTIPLE CHOICE QUESTIONS

Personal property (not real property) is also called _____.

A. codicil

B. apostile

C. escrow

D. chattel

A written instrument (except a will) used to create, transfer, surrender or assign an interest in real property is called _____.

A. a conveyance

B. a deposition

C. a jurat

D. an affirmation

MULTIPLE CHOICE ANSWERS

D. chattel

(Definitions)

Examples of personal property are clothing, cars, jewelry, etc.

A. a conveyance

(Definitions)

An example is a deed.

MULTIPLE CHOICE QUESTIONS

The authentication attached by the Department of State to a notarized document that is county-certified for possible international use is called _____.

A. a lien

B. a codicil

C. an apostile

D. an affirmation

A _____ is an instrument attached to a will that adds to or modifies the will.

A. judgment

B. apostile

C. chattel

D. codicil

MULTIPLE CHOICE ANSWERS

C. an apostile

(Definitions)

The document in question:

1. is notarized
2. is county-certified
3. contains the apostile (attached)

D. codicil

(Definitions)

The codicil is created after the creation of the will.

MULTIPLE CHOICE QUESTIONS

A(n) _____ is a person who is named in a will to carry out the will's provisions.

A. deponent

B. executor

C. jurat

D. affiant

A crime (other than a felony) is called _____.

A. a violation

B. a "C" misdemeanor

C. a petty offense

D. a misdemeanor

MULTIPLE CHOICE ANSWERS

B. executor

(Definitions)

If there is no will or no one is named in the will, then the court appoints an administrator.

D. a misdemeanor

(Definitions)

A crime is either a misdemeanor or a felony.

MULTIPLE CHOICE QUESTIONS

A _____ is a decree of a court which declares the amount of money which one party owes to another party.

A. apostile

B. judgment

C. jurat

D. codicil

A _____ is a claim or right to property which attaches to the specific property until a judgment (debt) is paid.

A. lien

B. conveyance

C. laches

D. chattel

MULTIPLE CHOICE ANSWERS

B. judgment

(Definitions)

A judgment can be final or temporary.

A. lien

(Definitions)

Liens may be filed at the county clerk's office.

MULTIPLE CHOICE QUESTIONS

The term _____ can be used interchangeably with "affiant."

A. litigator

B. guardian

C. deponent

D. juror

A verbal pledge by a person that his statements are true is known as an _____.

A. apostile

B. oath

C. authentication

D. lien

MULTIPLE CHOICE ANSWERS

C. deponent

(Definitions)

The deponent swears an oath to a written statement
or "affirms."

B. oath

(Definitions)

An oath cannot be administered over the telephone and must
be done in a manner in accordance with statute.

MULTIPLE CHOICE QUESTIONS

A person who starts a civil action is called _____.

A. the defendant

B. the appellant

C. the plaintiff

D. the guardian

A written statement called _____ empowers a person to act for another person.

A. an authentication

B. an affirmation

C. an ex parte instrument

D. a power of attorney

MULTIPLE CHOICE ANSWERS

C. the plaintiff

(Definitions)

The person that the plaintiff sues is called the defendant.

D. a power of attorney

(Definitions)

The person designated can act for the other person but does not have the right to practice law.

MULTIPLE CHOICE QUESTIONS

The statute which prescribes the period during which a civil action or criminal prosecution may be started is the _____.

A. statute of frauds

B. statute of minorities

C. statute of limitations

D. None of the above.

A person who is legally in charge of the property of a minor person or legally in charge of the minor person's property is called _____.

A. a defendant

B. a juror

C. a plaintiff

D. a guardian

MULTIPLE CHOICE ANSWERS

C. statute of limitations
(Definitions)

If a case is not started within the prescribed period, then the case may be dismissed.

D. a guardian
(Definitions)

Guardians may also be appointed for people that are mentally or physically incapacitated.

MULTIPLE CHOICE QUESTIONS

Something of value (Example: chattel, personal services, money, etc.) given to induce someone to enter into a contract is called _____.

A. a deponent

B. a will

C. an affirmation

D. consideration

Which of the following statements is not correct?

A. Notaries are appointed by the Secretary of State.

B. The jurisdiction of notaries is the entire New York State.

C. Notaries are appointed for a 2 year term.

D. Notaries at time of appointment must be U.S. citizens.

MULTIPLE CHOICE ANSWERS

D. consideration
(Definitions)

Services and affection are also consideration.

C. Notaries are appointed for a 2 year term.
(Executive Law 130)

Notaries are appointed for a 4 year term.

MULTIPLE CHOICE QUESTIONS

A non-resident of NYS who accepts the office of NYS notary appoints the _____ as the person on whom process can be served in his behalf.

A. State Comptroller

B. Governor

C. Lieutenant Governor

D. Secretary of State

Which of the following choices is false?

The Secretary of State must satisfy himself that notary public applicants:

A. are of good moral character

B. have the equivalent of a common school education.

C. are familiar with duties and responsibilities of notaries public.

D. have a college education.

MULTIPLE CHOICE ANSWERS

D. Secretary of State

(Executive Law 130)

The Secretary of State also examines the qualifications of applicants for notary public.

D. have a college education.

(Executive Law 130)

Also, the education requirement does not apply when applicants are attorneys or certain court clerks.

MULTIPLE CHOICE QUESTIONS

Which of the following choices is false?

No person can be appointed a notary public if he has been convicted of any of the following:

A. illegally using, carrying or possessing a pistol.

B. making or possessing burglar's instruments.

C. entry of a building.

D. aiding escape from prison.

Notary public applicants must submit to _____ the application, oath of office, and their signature.

A. clerk of court

B. Secretary of State

C. State Comptroller

D. Attorney General of NYS

MULTIPLE CHOICE ANSWERS

C. entry of a building.
(Executive Law 130)

UNLAWFUL entry of a building.

B. Secretary of State
(Executive Law 131)

The officer who issues the notary public commission is the Secretary of State.

MULTIPLE CHOICE QUESTIONS

The Secretary of State shall receive a non-refundable application fee of $_____ from applicants for appointment.

A. $20

B. $40

C. $60

D. $90

A notary public I.D. card must indicate the appointee's name, address, county and _____.

A. social security number

B. commission term

C. date of birth

D. gender

MULTIPLE CHOICE ANSWERS

C. $60

(Executive Law 131)

No further fee has to be paid for the issuance of the notary public commission.

B. commission term

(Executive Law 131)

The fee for the issuance of a duplicate card is $10.

MULTIPLE CHOICE QUESTIONS

Which of the following choices is false?

The Secretary of State must submit to the county clerk where the appointee resides the following:

A. the commission, duly dated

B. certified copy or original oath of office

C. the official signature

D. $30 apportioned from the application fee.

Applicants for reappointment shall submit to _____ their application and oath of office and $60 fee.

A. the clerk of court

B. the Secretary of State

C. the county clerk

D. Attorney General

MULTIPLE CHOICE ANSWERS

D. $30 apportioned from the application fee.

(Executive Law 131)

The correct amount is $20.

C. the county clerk

(Executive Law 131)

The county clerk must send $40 to the Secretary of State.

MULTIPLE CHOICE QUESTIONS

Which of the following choices is the best answer?

An instrument with an authentication of the notarial signature shall:

A. be entitled to be read into evidence.

B. be entitled to be recorded in any county of NYS.

C. both A and B

D. Neither A nor B

A person removed from office of notary public who signs or executes an instrument as notary is guilty of_____.

A. a violation

B. a misdemeanor

C. a felony

D. an "A" felony

MULTIPLE CHOICE ANSWERS

C. both A and B

(Executive Law 133)

Note that the county clerk authenticates the signature on the basis of the certification of the signature that was filed.

B. a misdemeanor

(Executive Law 140)

Same applies for a person removed as commissioner of deeds.

MULTIPLE CHOICE QUESTIONS

Which of the following choices is false?

A notary public is authorized to:

A. administer oaths and affirmations.

B. take affidavits and depositions.

C. receive and certify acknowledgments or proofs of deeds.

D. act as a sheriff.

Generally, a notary public is entitled to the following fee for administering an oath and certifying the same:

A. $2

B. $4

C. $6

D. $12

MULTIPLE CHOICE ANSWERS

D. act as a sheriff.

(Executive Law 135)

Also, a notary public who is an attorney may administer an oath or affirmation to his client.

A. $2

(Executive Law 136)

Also, $2 for certifying an acknowledgment or proof of execution of a written instrument ($2 for one person, $2 for each additional person, $2 for swearing in each witness)

MULTIPLE CHOICE QUESTIONS

Which of the following is not correct?

A notary public shall print, write or stamp beneath his signature in black ink:

A. his name.

B. the words "Notary Public State of New York"

C. the name of the county in which he originally qualified.

D. his date of birth.

Which of the following statements is false?

Acknowledgment or proof within NYS of a conveyance of real property situated in NYS may be made anywhere in NYS before:

A. a justice of the supreme court.

B. an official examiner of title.

C. a notary public.

D. any municipal official.

MULTIPLE CHOICE ANSWERS

D. his date of birth.

(Executive Law 137)

Must write the date his **commission** expires.

D. any municipal official.

(Real Property Law 298)

Can also be made before an official referee.

MULTIPLE CHOICE QUESTIONS

Select the best answer:

An acknowledgment **within a district** where an officer is authorized to perform his official duties may be made before:

A. a judge, clerk of court, or mayor or recorder of a city only.

B. surrogate, special surrogate, or special county judge only.

C. county clerk or other recording officer of a county only.

D. A, B and C are all correct.

Choose the best answer:

An acknowledgment shall not be taken by any officer unless he knows or has satisfactory evidence that:

A. the person making it is the person described.

B. the person is the person who executed such instrument.

C. Neither A nor B are correct.

D. Both A and B are correct.

MULTIPLE CHOICE ANSWERS

D. A, B and C are all correct.

(Real Property Law 298)

May be made also before a commissioner of deeds (outside NYC) or commissioner of deed (within NYC).

D. Both A and B are correct.

(Real Property Law 303)

The notary must know the person or have satisfactory evidence as to the identity of the person.

MULTIPLE CHOICE QUESTIONS

Which of the following choices would be correct fill-ins in the following: "On the ____ day of ___ in the year ____."

A. Wednesday…week…2009

B. afternoon…April…2009

C. 6th…June…2009

D. last…the month…2008

Which of the following choices is most correct?

When authorized, a notary public shall be present when a safe deposit box is opened by the lessor. The notary public shall file with the lessor a certificate which states:

A. the date of the opening of the safe deposit box.

B. a list of the contents.

C. Both A and B are correct.

D. Neither A nor B are correct.

MULTIPLE CHOICE ANSWERS

C. 6th...June...2009

(Real Property Law 309)

Same applies to certificate of proof of execution by a subscribing witness.

C. Both A and B.

(Banking Law 335)

The certificate must contain:

1) the date of opening of the safe deposit box,

2) the name of the lessee, and

3) a list of the contents.

MULTIPLE CHOICE QUESTIONS

A person who violates the provisions of Judiciary Law 484 (Practicing as an attorney) shall be guilty of _____.

A. a violation

B. a misdemeanor

C. An "E" felony

D. a "B" felony

Which of the following statements is false?
An officer is not entitled to a fee for administering an oath to:

A. a teacher or college professor.

B. a member of the legislature.

C. to any military officer.

D. to an inspector of elections.

MULTIPLE CHOICE ANSWERS

B. a misdemeanor

(Judiciary Law 485)

Examples of such acts are the notary public presenting himself as an attorney or preparing wills, codicils, or pleadings of any kind.

A. a teacher or college professor.

(Public Officers Law)

Also, cannot collect a fee from a clerk of the poll, or from any public officer or public employee while in the performance of their duties.

MULTIPLE CHOICE QUESTIONS

Which of the following choices is the best answer?

A notary may be removed from office for:

A. practicing fraud or deceit.

B. making a misstatement of a material fact in the application for appointment.

C. Both A and B are correct.

D. Neither A nor B are correct.

A notary public in exercising his powers under this article must in addition to the venue and signature print, typewrite, or stamp beneath his signature in _____ ink, his name, the words "Notary Public State of New York," the name of the county in which he originally qualified and date upon which his commission expires.

A. blue (only)

B. black (only)

C. black or blue

D. black, blue or green

MULTIPLE CHOICE ANSWERS

C. Both A and B are correct.

(Executive Law)

Also may be removed for preparing and taking an oath of an affiant to a statement the notary knew to be false or fraudulent.

B. black (only)

(Executive Law 137)

PRACTICE EXAM #1

Instructions: Answer the following 40 questions based on New York State statutes relating to notaries public and the information contained in the publication "Notary Public License Law" issued by the New York State Department of State Division of Licensing Services.

1. Which of the following statements is not correct?

A. The fee for a notary public commission is $60.

B. The Secretary of State commissions notaries public.

C. The term of a notary public commission is 2 years.

D. Notary public examinations are scheduled throughout NYS.

2. Notaries public are commissioned in _____.

A. their city of residence.

B. the city where they are employed.

C. their county of residence.

D. their town or village of residence.

3. Which of the following statements is not correct?

No person shall be appointed as a notary public who has been convicted of _____ .

A. making or possessing burglar's weapons.

B. any felony.

C. unlawful entry of a building.

D. any misdemeanor.

4. The county clerk and register of any county with whom a certificate of official character has been filed shall collect for the filing _____.

A. $2

B. $4

C. $5

D. $10

5. A notary public who is removed from office and then executes any instrument as a notary public is guilty of a _____.

A. violation

B. petty offense

C. misdemeanor

D. felony.

6. Which of the following is not eligible for the office of notary public?

A. commissioner of elections

B. sheriff

C. member of the legislature

D. inspector of elections

7. Generally, the fee for an oath or affirmation is:

A. $2

B. $4

C. $5

D. $10

8. The signature and seal of a county clerk upon a certificate of official character of a notary public may be:

1. facsimile

2. printed

3. stamped

4. photographed or engraved thereon

A. Only 1, 2 and 3 are correct.

B. Only 2 and 3 are correct.

C. 1, 2, 3 and 4 are all correct.

D. Only 3 is correct.

9. Which of the following statements is not correct?

A NYS notary public is:

A. authorized to administer oaths and affirmations.

B. not authorized to administer an oath to himself.

C. not authorized to administer oaths and affirmations.

D. authorized to receive and certify acknowledgments.

10. A notary public who is an attorney at law admitted to practice in NYS may:

1. administer an oath or affirmation to his client.

2. take the affidavit or acknowledgment of his client.

A. Both 1 and 2 are not correct.

B. Only 1 is correct.

C. Only 2 is correct.

D. Both 1 and 2 are correct.

11. A person who holds himself out to be a notary public but is not, or a notary public who commits fraud or deceit in the performance of his duties, is guilty of _____.

A. a petty offense

B. a misdemeanor

C. a felony

D. None of the above.

12. The term "conveyance" includes written instruments by which any estate or interest in _____ property is created, transferred, mortgaged or assigned.

1. personal

2. real

A. Only 1 is correct.

B. Only 2 is correct.

C. Neither 1 nor 2 is correct.

D. Both 1 and 2 are correct.

13. An officer authorized to take the acknowledgment or proof of a conveyance who is guilty of fraudulent practice or malfeasance in the execution of any duty prescribed by law in relation to it is

_____.

A. guilty of a petty offense.

B. liable for a statutory fine of $150.00.

C. liable in damages to the person injured.

D. None of the above.

14. When the lessor (bank) of a safe deposit box opens the safe deposit box in front of a notary public (pursuant to Banking Law 335), the notary shall file with the lessor a certificate under seal which contains:

   1. the date of the opening of the safe deposit box.

   2. the name of the lessee.

   3. a list (inventory) of the contents.

A. 1 only

B. 1 and 2 only

C. 1, 2 and 3

D. 3 only

15. The rule which authorizes a deposition to be taken before a notary public in a civil proceeding is found in:

A. Criminal Procedure Law

B. NYS Administrative Code.

C. Family Court Act.

D. Civil Practice Law and Rules

16. Which of the following statements is correct?

A. A notary public may in certain situations practice law.

B. A notary public may prepare a will.

C. A notary public shall not practice law.

D. None of the above.

17. A notary public subjects himself to the following for asking or receiving more than the statutory allowance for administering an oath in connection with an affidavit.

  1. criminal prosecution

  2. civil lawsuit

  3. removal from office

A. 3 only

B. 1 and 3 only

C. 1, 2 and 3

D. 2 only

18. A sentence of imprisonment for a Class "A" misdemeanor is a definite sentence which shall not exceed_____.

A. 6 months

B. 1 year

C. 3 years

D. 7 years

19. A person appointed by the court to manage the estate of a dead person who died without a will or who did not name such a person in the will is _____.

A. an executor

B. a plaintiff

C. an administrator

D. a deponent

20. A person who signs his signature on an affidavit is called _____.

A. the plaintiff

B. the legatee

C. the executor

D. the affiant

21. If a person declines to take an oath because of religious reasons, he may make _____.

A. a codicil

B. an affirmation

C. a contract

D. a lien

22. "Sworn to before me this _____ day of _____, 2010" is referred to as:

A. a lien

B. a contract

C. a jurat

D. a codicil

23. Something that has value and is given to induce someone to enter into a contract is called_____.

A. real property

B. chattel

C. will

D. consideration

24. A person who starts a civil lawsuit is called _____.

A. the antagonist

B. the defendant

C. the appellant

D. the plaintiff

25. The law which specifies the time during which a civil action or criminal prosecution must be started is called:

A. The Statute of Frauds

B. The Law of Venue

C. The Statute of Limitations

D. None of the above.

26. The geographical place where an affidavit is taken by a notary or commissioner of deeds is called the _____.

A. locale

B. town

C. venue

D. venison

27. The total commission fee for the appointment of a notary public is _____.

A. $20

B. $40

C. $60

D. None of the above.

28. The fee for swearing in a witness is _____.

A. $.75

B. $2.00

C. $2.50

D. $4.00

29. The county clerk fee for issuance of Certificate of Official Character is _____.

A. $2

B. $4

C. $5

D. None of the above.

30. The fee for an authentication certificate is _____.

A. $2

B. $3

C. $4

D. $6

31. A newly commissioned notary public has an office next to that of a law firm. The notary public may:

A. advertise that he gives legal advice.

B. agree to divide his fees with the law firm.

C. give legal advice.

D. None of the above.

32. The Secretary of State is not authorized to issue a duplicate notary public I.D. card _____.

A. to replace a destroyed card.

B. to replace a damaged card.

C. to replace a lost card.

D. to be kept as a spare I.D. card.

33. Which of the following choices is not correct?

If a notary public is removed from office _____.

A. he is thereafter not eligible to be appointed a notary public.

B. he is not authorized to administer oaths.

C. he is guilty of a felony if he continues to act as a notary public.

D. he cannot sign or execute any instrument as a notary public.

34. Which of the following three defects would render an official certificate by a notary public invalid?

1. The term of the notary was expired at the time of issuing the notarial certificate.

2. The name of the notary is misspelled on his identification card.

3. The notary failed to file his official oath.

A. 1 only

B. 2 only

C. 3 only

D. None. These defects do not render the certificate invalid.

35. A notary public who is guilty of malfeasance or fraudulent practice in the execution of a duty prescribed by law is:

A. liable for a fine of $100.

B. liable for a fine of $500.

C. liable for a fine of $1,500.

D. liable in damages to the person injured.

36. A law enacted by the New York State legislature is called:

A. a codicil

B. a seal

C. an attestation

D. a statute

37. Which of the following two statements are correct?

A notary public may:

1. solemnize a marriage

2. take the acknowledgment of parties and witnesses to a written contract of marriage

A. Only 1 is correct.

B. Only 2 is correct.

C. Both 1 and 2 are correct.

D. None. Both 1 and 2 are incorrect.

38. A notary public may:

A. prepare a will or a codicil

B. prepare a deed or an assignment

C. prepare a mortgage

D. None of the above.

39. A notary is asked by a person to notarize an affidavit. Which of the following is correct?

A. The notary can negotiate a fee.

B. The notary must charge a fee of $20.

C. The notary may charge a fee of $10.

D. None of the above.

40. If a party violates the provisions of Judiciary Law 67 (Fees of Public Officers) he is liable to the person aggrieved _____.

A. for damages plus $300.

B. for damages plus travelling expenses.

C. for treble damages.

D. None of the above.

ANSWERS: PRACTICE EXAM #1:

1. C...Executive Law 130. The term is 4 years

2. C...Executive Law 131. Their county of residence.

3. D...Executive Law 130. Can be appointed if convicted of a misdemeanor.

4. D...Executive Law 132. Also, for ISSUING a certificate of official character, the county clerk shall collect $5.

5. C... Executive Law 140. In addition, a notary public who is removed from office is not eligible to be appointed again.

6. B... NYS Constitution, Article 13, Section 13(a). Also, a person convicted of any felony or certain specified crimes is not eligible for the office of notary public.

7. A...Executive Law 136. This is the fee unless another fee is prescribed by statute.

8. C…Executive Law 134. All are correct.

9. C…Executive Law 135. Notaries public ARE authorized to administer oaths and affirmations.

10. D…Executive Law 135. He may do so in respect to any matter, claim, action or proceeding.

11. B…Executive Law 135-a. (a misdemeanor)

12. B…(Real Property Law 290.

13. C…Real Property Law 330. (liable in damages to the person injured).

14. C…Banking Law 335 (1, 2 and 3) Also, within 10 days of the opening of the safe deposit box, a copy of this certificate must be mailed to the lessee at his last known postal address….

15. D…Civil Practice Law and Rules.

16. C… Judiciary Law 484.

17. C…Public Officers Law 67 (Opinion of Attorney General)

18. B… Legal terms. The term of imprisonment for misdemeanor is up to and including a year.

19. C…Legal Terms

20. D…Legal Terms

21. B…Legal Terms

22. C…Legal Terms

23. D…Legal Terms

24. D…Legal Terms

25. C…Legal Terms

26. C…Legal Terms

27. C…Executive Law 131

28. B…Schedule of Fees

29. C…Schedule of Fees

30. B…Schedule of Fees

31. D…Judiciary Law 484. Notaries public are expressly prohibited from practicing law or dividing their fees with attorneys.

32. D…Executive Law 131

33. C…Executive Law 140. He is guilty of a MISDEMEANOR.

34. D …Executive Law 142-a

35. D…Real Property Law 330

36. D…Legal Terms

37. D…Domestic Relations Law 484.

38. D…Judiciary Law 484

39. D…Executive Law 136 and Public Officers Law 67. Fee is $2.

40. C…Judiciary Law 67. Also, liability for treble damages is in addition to any other punishment for the criminal offense prescribed by law.

Brief Note:

Now that you have completed the first practice exam, it might be a good idea to review any sections that you found difficult.

After you are confident that you have done a diligent review, take the second exam for further practice.

(Remember, we have tried to make the questions difficult to bring out any areas where you would benefit from further study.)

PRACTICE EXAM #2

Instructions: Answer the following 40 questions based on New York State statutes relating to notaries public and the information contained in the publication "Notary Public License Law" issued by the New York State Department of State Division of Licensing Services.

1. Which of the following four choices relating to these two statements is most correct?

1. "Do you solemnly swear that the contents of this affidavit subscribed by you is correct and true?"

2. "Do you solemnly, sincerely and truly declare and affirm that the statements made by you are correct?"

A. 1 and 2 are affirmations.

B. 1 and 2 are oaths.

C. 1 is an affirmation; 2 is an oath.

D. 1 is an oath; 2 is an affirmation.

2. Which of the following statements is not correct?

A. A notary shall not give advice on the law.

B. A notary may not ask for and get legal business to send to a lawyer from whom he receives consideration for sending business.

C. A notary may divide his fees with a lawyer.

D. A notary may be married or unmarried.

3. A notary may take an acknowledgment of a party_____.

A. only if party is present or is communicating by telephone.

B. only if party is communicating by videophone or is present.

C. only if party is present.

D. None of the above.

4. A notary public who is a non-resident of NYS and who ceases to have an office or place of business in NYS _____.

A. may continue to serve as a notary public for one year.

B. may continue to serve as a notary public until the expiration of his term.

C. may continue to serve as a notary public upon the payment of a $60 fee.

D. vacates his office as a notary.

5. The Secretary of State may not remove from office for misconduct any notary appointed by him unless the person:

1. is served with a copy of the charges against him.

2. has had an opportunity to be heard.

A. 1 only is correct.

B. 2 only is correct.

C. Both 1 and 2 are not correct.

D. Both 1 and 2 are correct.

6. The acknowledgment or proof of a conveyance of real property within the state or any other written instrument may be made:

1. by a married woman

2. by an unmarried woman

A. Only 1 is correct.

B. Only 2 is correct.

C. Both 1 and 2 are correct.

D. 1 is correct and 2 is correct only if over the age of 25.

7. A person convicted of a _____ in NYS or any other state or territory shall not be appointed a notary public.

A. misdemeanor

B. "A" misdemeanor

C. felony

D. petty offense

8. Which of the following is not correct?

A notary public card contains the following:

A. appointee's name

B. address and county

C. social security number

D. commission term

9. The fee for a duplicate notary public identification card is:

A. $2

B. $5

C. $10

D. $60

10. Who may not certify as to the official character of a notary public?

A. Secretary of State

B. county clerk of county in which the commission of a notary public is filed.

C. county clerk where a notary filed his autograph signature and certificate of official character.

D. a mayor of a city with a population of over 100,000.

11. Which of following are eligible for the office of notary public?

1. sheriff

2. commissioner of elections

3. a member of the legislature

A. 1, 2 and 3

B. 1 and 2 only

C. 3 only

D. 2 and 3 only

12. Every notary public duly qualified is authorized within _____ to administer oaths and affirmations.

A. the county where commissioned only

B. the county of residence only

C. New York State

D. None of the above

13. The fee for taking and certifying the acknowledgment or proof of execution of a written instrument by one person is _____.

A. $2

B. $4

C. $.75

D. None of the above.

14. A notary public who is duly licensed as an attorney may substitute the words _____ for the words "Notary Public."

A. "Certified Notary Public."

B. "Expert Notary Public."

C. "Lawyer."

D. "Attorney and Counselor at Law."

15. An officer authorized to take the acknowledgment of a conveyance or other instrument who is guilty of malfeasance or fraudulent practice in the execution of any duty prescribed by law in relation thereto is liable in damages to _____.

A. the Secretary of State

B. county clerk

C. state comptroller

D. the person injured

16. For a conveyance to be recorded:

A. the conveyance may be in any language without a translation.

B. the conveyance may be in any language without a translation as long as it is written in English letters or characters.

C. a fee of $25 must be paid.

D. None of the above.

17. Within ___days of the opening of a safe deposit box pursuant to Banking Law 335, a copy of the certificate of the notary public shall be mailed to the lessee (the renter of the safe deposit box) at his last known postal address.

A. 5

B. 10

C. 20

D. 30

18.A notary guilty of official misconduct is guilty of:

A. an "A" misdemeanor

B. a "B" misdemeanor

C. a "D" felony

D. an "E" felony

19. Which of the following is correct? A notary public

A. has authority to solemnize marriages.

B. may take the acknowledgment of parties to a written contract of marriage.

C. may take the acknowledgment of witnesses to a written contract of marriage.

D. has no authority to solemnize marriages.

20. A proceeding to punish for criminal contempt a person who unlawfully practices law may be instituted:

1. on the court's motion.

2. on motion of any officer charged with the duty of investigating or prosecuting unlawful practice of law.

3. by any bar association of NYS.

A. 1 and 3 only

B. 2 and 3 only

C. 1 and 2 only

D. 1, 2 and 3

21. An officer who violates the provisions of Public Officers Law, Section 67 (Fees of Public Officers) in addition to the punishment prescribed by law for the criminal offense, is liable in behalf of the person aggrieved for _____.

A. 100% of the damages.

B. 200% of the damages.

C. 300% of the damages.

D. None of the above.

22. Which of the following is not correct?

An officer is not entitled to a fee for administering an oath of office to:

A. a member of the legislature.

B. a military officer.

C. an inspector of elections.

D. a general of the Knights of Columbus.

23. A notary public who knowingly issues a false certificate is guilty of:

A. an "A" misdemeanor

B. a "B" misdemeanor

C. a "D" felony

D. an "E" felony

24. A signed statement that is sworn to by the creator in front of a notary public is called _____.

A. a codicil

B. a lien

C. a contract

D. an affidavit

25. A _____ is the section on an affidavit where a notary certifies that the statement was sworn to in front of him.

A. codicil

B. appendix

C. preamble

D. jurat

26. A claim or legal right which attaches to specific property until a debt owed is paid is called_____.

A. a misdemeanor

B. a lien

C. a statute

D. a deposition

27. A crime that is not a felony is called _____.

A. a petty offense

B. a violation

C. a traffic infraction

D. a misdemeanor

28. The fee for swearing in a witness is ____.

A. $2

B. $4

C. $6

D. $5

29. The county clerk fee for issuance of a Certificate of Official Character is ____.

A. $2

B. $4

C. $6

D. $5

30. The fee for an authentication certificate is _____.

A. $2

B. $3

C. $4

D. $6

31. A notary public maintains an office in New York State but lives in New Jersey. The notary public:

A. is not allowed to administer oaths in New York State.

B. may only take acknowledgments in New Jersey.

C. is deemed to have appointed the Secretary of State as the person upon whom process can be served on his behalf.

D. None of the above.

32. A notary public commissioned in Kings County wishes to file his autograph signature in other counties so that county clerks may certify as to his official character. The notary public may file his autograph signature and certificate of official character:

A. only in the other four New York City counties.

B. only in counties adjoining Kings county.

C. in every county of New York State.

D. None of the above.

33. Which of the following is not correct?

A. Venue is the area where the notary takes an acknowledgment.

B. The venue is listed at the beginning of an instrument.

C. An affidavit does not have to show the venue on its face.

D. None of the above.

34. Which of the following four persons are eligible to be appointed a notary public?

   1. a commissioner of elections

   2. an inspector of elections

   3. a member of the legislature

   4. a sheriff

A. 1 and 2 only

B. 1, 2 and 3 only

C. 1, 2, 3 and 4

D. 4 only

35. Which of the following statements is not correct?

A. All single women may make a conveyance of property.

B. All married women may make a conveyance of property.

C. A single woman may only make a conveyance of property if she is over the age of twenty-five.

D. A married woman may make a conveyance of property same as a single woman.

36. For a conveyance of real property to be recorded:

   1. it must be in the English language in all cases.

   2. proper names must be in foreign characters.

A. Only 1 is correct.

B. Both 1 and 2 are correct.

C. Only 2 is correct.

D. Both 1 and 2 are not correct.

37. Which of the following is false?

A notary public may be removed from office for:

A. practicing fraud.

B. making a willful misstatement of a material fact in the notary public application for appointment.

C. taking an oath to a statement the notary knew to be fraudulent.

D. committing a petty offense.

38. An authentication by Department of State attached to a county-certified document to be used internationally is called _____.

A. a certified copy

B. an attestation

C. an apostile

D. None of the above.

39. Total commission fee for the office of notary public is $60 ($___ is for the appointment and $___ is for the filing of oath of office).

A. $30...$30

B. $10...$50

C. $40...$20

D. $35...$25

40. Which of the following choices is not correct with respect to the opening of a safe deposit box pursuant to Banking Law 335?

A. 30 days notice has to be given to the lessee.

B. List of contents must be filed with lessor by notary public.

C. A copy of notarial certificate must be mailed to the lessor.

D. Lessor must open the safe deposit box in the presence of the notary public.

ANSWERS: PRACTICE EXAM #2

1. D...as per case law.

2. C...as per Notary Public License Law booklet from Division of Licensing Services.

3. C...as per Notary Public License Law booklet from Division of Licensing Services.

4. D...Executive Law 130

5. D...Executive Law 130

6. C...Real Property Law 302

7. C...Executive Law 130

8. C...Executive Law 131

9. C...Executive Law 131

10. D...Executive Law 132

11. D...NYS Constitution Article 13, Section 13(a)

12. C...Executive Law 135

13. A...Executive Law 136

14. D...Executive Law 137

15. D...Real Property Law 330

16. D...Real Property Law 333

17. B...Banking Law 335

18. A...Penal Law 175.40

19. D...Domestic Relations Law 11

20. D...Judiciary Law 750

21. C...Public Officers Law 67

22. D...Public Officers Law 69

23. A...Penal Law 175.40

24. D...Legal Terms

25. D...Legal Terms

26. B...Legal Terms

27. D...Legal Definitions

28. A...Schedule of Fees

29. D...Schedule of Fees

30. B...Schedule of Fees

31. C...Executive Law 130

32. C...Executive Law 132

33. C...Legal Terms

34. B...Executive Laws, 3-200, 3-400, and Public Law 3, County Law 534, and New York State Constitution, Article 3, Section 7, and Article 13 (a).

35. C...Executive Law 302

36. D...Real Property Law 333

37. D...Executive Law 135-a

38. C...Legal Terms

39. C...Schedule of Fees

40. C...Banking Law 335. Must be mailed to the **lessee**.

PASS THE NOTARY EXAM - NEW YORK STATE
COMPUTER PROGRAM

This new computer program contains all of the material in this book, along with interactive features which make learning both easy and fun! The program is designed to be fast and simple.

It includes a 'Quick Program Tour' which displays all the screens in the program, including the 'Home Page Screen' which has 6 buttons to take you to the 6 parts of the program.

The "Notary Exam' button explains the Notary Exam..

The 'Quick Questions' button takes you to hundreds of T/F Questions where you can practice with interactive flash cards.

The 'Multiple choice screen provides extra practice. The multiple choice questions will make you think hard and remember better. It has a review feature for any questions you answer incorrectly.

The program also remembers the Quick Questions that you answer incorrectly so that you may review them in 'My Difficult Questions' section. This encourages you to study the questions that you find difficult. Once the program determines that you are answering a difficult question correctly, it will remove it from the 'My Difficult Questions' section.

FAST AND EASY AND FUN!

You can download the program and start using this valuable tool immediately or you can order the CD by mail.

Either way, you will be pleasantly surprised by its ease of use and effectiveness. Learn more about this inexpensive and helpful study tool at:

www.NotaryProgram.com

INDEX

Made in the USA
Lexington, KY
26 June 2013